VERBAL
KUNG FU

For Freelancers
Master the Art of Defense Against Difficult Clients

verbal kung fu for freelancers / Jeremy Tuber.
ISBN 978-0-9816220-4-0

Table of Contents

Table of Contents Cont...

SECTION I:
Introduction

*"A quarrel is quickly settled when deserted
by one party; there is no battle
unless there be two."*

**— Seneca , 4 B.C. - 65 A.D.,
Spanish-born Roman Statesman, philosopher**

Introduction

What is Verbal Kung Fu for Freelancers?

Why did I write this book?

- Do you feel clients try to take advantage of you?

- Does it bother you when they try to get things as cheaply as possible?

- Do you get frustrated when you realize that giving in or getting angry are both bad options?

For me the answers were once: yes, yes and yes again! That's why I wrote this book.

I've met and had the privilege of working with some wonderful clients over the years as a freelance graphic designer. But like everyone else who's freelanced, I've had some bad clients as well. When I first started freelancing I assumed that everyone I worked for would be fair, honest and cooperative, but it didn't take me long to realize that not everyone was like this.

I found that some clients can be downright rude, demanding, untruthful and deceptive. I further found that the more generous I was with some clients, the more they tried to take. I've had a client look me straight in the eyes and tell me, "*My goal is to get as much out of you for as little money as possible.*" Unbelievable — what a jerk. Sadly, I've found a lot of clients can be like this; they just don't bluntly admit it like this jackass did.

From talking with freelancers over the years I quickly found this wasn't an isolated problem — everyone seems to have the same gripe, but no one had a solution to it! Visit any freelancing message board and you'll find it littered with messages of disgruntled people who've been burned or are being burned by unfair clients. Talk to any freelancer in the business and you'll find they have a *"client from hell"* story.

After speaking to an alumni group at a job fair at the Art Institute of Phoenix, I learned that while students are educated on some basic strategies in business, they have no practical training when it comes to dealing with clients. I feel badly for these kids. They're looking to take on the world as freelancers but they have no idea what they're in for... and they don't have the confidence or experience to deal with what's coming. Most aspiring freelancers end up learning the hard way: by making mistakes and trying to learn from them, just like I did.

So we've got freelancers in the industry that are frustrated and aspiring freelancers that are in for a really rude surprise (no, not all clients are nice). Either way, not knowing how to deal with difficult clients can, and often does leave freelancers jaded, burned out and sometimes broke. I have my own share of rotten client stories, but some good did come out of those experiences — it fueled the fire to write this book:

The question isn't if you'll run into a difficult client, but when.

1. I was sick and tired of clients bullying me, walking over me and trying every trick in the book to take advantage of the situation. One stressed me out so much I ended up in the hospital — the jackass was calling me as early as 6:30 AM and as late as 11:00 PM.

2. There are too many other freelancers, just like you, that are faced with this same problem. I just felt it was time that someone stepped up and provided a solution on how to handle difficult clients instead of just complaining. I thought, "Why not me?"

3. I want to help as many freelancers worldwide build the confidence to tackle any difficult or demanding client. Life is to short to work with crappy clients. Freelancers should have the chance to enjoy their freedom and their career — I am hoping you find this book will help you do this.

What's the story behind Verbal Kung Fu for Freelancers?

Is being railroaded by clients just part of business?

I had my share of uncomfortable run-ins with clients as a new freelancer — verbal exchanges that left me feeling taken advantage of and angry. The problem was I didn't know what to do about it. Other freelancers told me that *"This was just part of business and that every freelancer has a bad client from time to time. The best way is to just get through it as soon as possible."*

I didn't buy it.

I couldn't accept that being taken advantage by opportunistic people was *"just part of business"*, and if it was I didn't want to be a freelancer.

Fortunately I learned that freelancing wasn't about letting the client get whatever she / he wanted.

The First Sensei

In about my second year freelancing I was introduced to a business strategist, former Air Force dog trainer, drummer and professional photographer named Bill Gluth.

After Bill helped me develop my business and marketing strategy I had the opportunity to work with him on some co-development projects: Bill did strategy, I did design.

As Bill and I worked on more projects together, I had the opportunity to see how he handled clients that got confused, asked for more than what they paid for, or just got down-right demanding.

After all, Bill's a freelancer too — he's just a business strategist instead of graphic artist, web designer or other creative industry pro.

Here's what Bill was hearing, do they sound familiar to you as well?

- Why aren't my sales figures up?
  Are you sure your marketing strategy is working?

- I talked with my friend and she disagrees that I need to have a web site right now, are you sure of your advice?

- I need you to come up with some free marketing ideas for me before I decide to hire you.

- I need you to make some changes to the content I sent you.

- I'll be able to pay your fee as soon as my customers pay me.

I learned that Bill heard the same type of nonsense from clients as I and other freelancers did, but I quickly found out that he had the wisdom, the experience and the confidence to know how to handle it. Bill just had a way with clients. It was difficult to explain at first; I just remember noting that even when clients got out of line or tried to take advantage of the situation, he always knew just what to say without being either a doormat or a war hawk.

Bill had the uncanny knack of being able to steer clients in a particular direction but still made them feel good about it (cooperation rather than confrontation). For you Star Wars geeks like me, it was like Obi Wan Kenobi using the "*Jedi mind trick*" on the Imperial Storm Troopers.

A rare combination of logic, empathy, psychology and perhaps a pinch of magic — this guy was a master at powerfully communicating with clients while avoiding being taken advantage of. Much like a young Luke Skywalker in Star Wars, I found myself wide-eyed and jaw-dropped, eager to learn this new skill. I invested a lot of time trying to figure out what Bill was doing and how in the heck he was doing it! This was when I first realized that being taken advantage of was NOT part of freelancing - there was a better way!

After my initial amazement wore off, and I had the opportunity to work with a few more clients with Bill it finally dawned on me — I could probably use this approach with my own clients.
Perhaps I should probably start writing down just about everything that came out of his mouth when he's talking to clients. This idea took longer to pop into my brain than I care to admit, had I thought of it earlier it would have saved me loads of aggravation.

From that point on I wrote down everything that Bill said in regards to dealing with clients, at least as much of it as I could — the guy talks really fast. Additionally, I'd ask him, "*If a client said this... how would you respond?*" I was starting the foundations of *Verbal Kung Fu for Freelancers*, but I didn't know it at the time. Bill was the sensei (master), and I was the student.

At first all of this felt a little like learning a foreign language: clumsy and slow. In fact, several times I had to ask Bill if he'd repeat or further explain something so I got it down on paper correctly. It wasn't frustrating though, it was actually exciting. I was on to something big (that would help a lot of folks) but I just didn't know what.

I would go back later and study what Bill had said, and after a while I started to see a pattern develop of how he was influencing clients in a gentle, non-confrontational way. I started to make sense of what Bill was doing. I found the more I became familiar with how Bill was communicating with clients, the more I felt comfortable and confident that I could use the same approach in some of the difficult situations clients were putting me in.

It was like a door to a new room in my mind had just opened up and said, "*Come on in!*"

Well, of course we all know that theory in a vacuum doesn't always hold up in the real world with real clients. Even though Bill's approach to his clients sounded good, and what I wrote down on paper looked good, it still didn't mean it would work on my clients, but I gave it a shot anyway.

But it did work — it works incredibly well in "*real world*" with "*real clients*"; even for a non-confrontational, introvert like me!

As I honed my skills, what was really intriguing to me was that I quickly found I could apply Bill's influential but non-confrontational approach to other areas of my life as well (especially in my personal life with family and friends). Furthermore, I could share it with other people who were having the same challenges I was. It was at this point I felt I had something big to share with people, but I didn't know what it was or what to call it.

So where does the "Kung Fu" fit in?

While I was learning this new skill from Bill that would help me develop more confidence in handling difficult clients, a real sensei of a local dojo asked me to design a web site for his martial arts business. He taught a Japanese form of martial arts called, "Aikido" (this is the martial art Steven Segal practices if you're not familiar with it).

I'd never heard of aikido before meeting this sensei; in fact, I'd been boxing for a number of years, but this approach to combat was completely new. In payment for doing his web site, the sensei invited me to join his class as a new student — since I was already in the mode of learning new things, I figured I'd give it a shot.

Instead of a sport like boxing that often matches brute force and aggression to beat down an opponent, aikido uses circular, fluid motions to use an opponent's energy against him. I was amazed at how aikido black belts could quickly and effortlessly gain control of an opponent (no matter how big or strong) just by grabbing an arm or a wrist. Just as amazing, when the black belt released the opponent from his control, there wasn't any damage done to the opponent, other than perhaps wounded pride.

After being in the class for a few months I found that the essence aikido is about being able defending yourself efficiently and gracefully — not caving in or being afraid of people, and not aggressively attacking them either (like punching someone in the eye like boxing). Aikido was an ideal way for non-combative, non-confrontational people to defend themselves against an antagonist. Sounds a lot like Bill's approach to handing clients, doesn't it?

Verbal Kung Fu for Freelancers was created from the teachings of these two masters: Bill's approach to dealing with difficult clients and my aikido sensei's approach to clashing with hostile opponents. It's a professional, powerful but non-combative way of standing up for yourself when a client becomes verbally aggressive, demanding or unrealistic. No more fight or flight modes where you feel pressure to comply with your clients, or aggressively confronting them so they don't take advantage of you — your clients won't know what hit 'em.

So, if you're ready young student, tie on your white belt. Let's get your training started...

Okay, then how did I get *kung fu* instead of *aikido*? Of course aikido would have been nice since that was the art I'd learned but most people think aikido is a form of origami and they spell it, *"Ikeedo"*, which makes it difficult for people to remember your web address. I decided on Kung Fu since it was easier to spell and remember.

Are clients born rotten, become rotten or don't even know they are rotten?

There are some clients that are unfair/demanding because that's just the way they are; it's part of their personality. Perhaps they are just not nice people. There can be any number of other reasons why they are behaving like this, but I've found that most of the time clients behave this way because they feel it will help them get what they want. This often boils down to greed and selfishness — sometimes mixed with client ignorance.

Don't get me wrong, this isn't the norm for most clients. But if you've been a freelancer for any amount of time, you've run across some of these *"tough customers"*. Calling them *"tough customers"* is a nice euphemism for these folks — they are often called MUCH worse by frustrated freelancers that have had enough of them!

Clients, whether intentionally or unintentionally test our boundaries as freelancers and often try to get as much out of us as they can. Like any other group of people in society, there are good clients and not-so-good clients. Since you never know what type of client you'll end up working for, you absolutely have to know how to effectively defend yourself against the not-so-good ones.

Non-effective techniques for handling difficult clients

Whenever conflicts with a client arise, freelancers feel trapped in a fight or flight mode. It's not a fun position to be in. Thoughts race in your mind: *"What do I say, and how in the heck do I get out of this?"*

You can take a submissive tone towards the client and just comply with his or her wishes: *"I guess that's okay..."* But your client has taken advantage of you, which isn't fair. Freelancers that are non-confrontational typically take this approach, which is called the *Compliant Child* by some sales training professionals. Whatever you want to call it, it's not a good approach because it leaves you feeling used and unappreciated.

If you choose to fight and dig in your heels, (in contrast to the *Compliant Child*) this approach is called the *Rebellious Child*. With this approach you might respond with, *"I don't do that"*, or *"I'll have to charge you."* And while you've stopped your client from potentially taking advantage of you, there's a good chance you've offended them by taking this approach — and you'll lose the client! No one wants to hear things like, *"That's not my policy"*, or *"You should have read your contract."* So neither approach is all that effective.

In both of the examples listed above: avoiding conflict or taking a hard stance — the result is not effective for you or your client. Both offer a win-lose situation where one party feels good about the outcome and the other feels bad. The question then might be, *"Is it possible to create a win-win situation where all parties feel good about the outcome?"* For almost all freelancers, this poses a big problem: being able to stand up and defend yourself, but avoid getting confrontational and possibly losing a client.

When faced with this dilemma, the client is going to expect you to either go into the *Compliant Child* or the *Rebellious Child* role: you're either going to comply with their wishes or dig your heels in and fight. I am going to help you change the rules and stand your ground without any fear of losing your client — it's called *Verbal Kung Fu for Freelancers*.

Keep reading eager student; you have now graduated from white belt to yellow belt. Yellow is better... except when eating snow... don't eat yellow snow.

Congratulations.

How much more grievous are the consequences of anger than the causes of it.

— **Marcus Aurelius**
121-80 AD, Roman
Emperor, Philosopher

命

SECTION II:
Becoming a Master of
Verbal Kung Fu for Freelancers

*"You'll be able to spit nails, kid. Like the guy
says, you're gonna eat lightning and you're
gonna crap thunder. You're gonna become a
very dangerous person."*

— Mickey, from the movie, "Rocky"

Becoming a Master of Verbal Kung Fu for Freelancers

Learn the Basics

If you jump in and just approach this resource as a bunch of phrases you need to memorize to manipulate your client, you may be disappointed. *Verbal Kung Fu for Freelancers* isn't a bunch of zingers you recite in front of a client to get them to do what you want; it's a way of reframing what you say and how you say it to gain cooperation and avoid conflict.

In fact, you'll find that this philosophy can easily be applied to other relationships in your life.

If you learn the philosophy and the background techniques for how to deal with conflict you won't need to memorize phrases.

Practice Makes Perfect

You've heard this phase before. It's true. Whether it's martial arts, sales calls, making presentations or designing logos — you've got to practice to become proficient. *Verbal Kung Fu for Freelancers* is a lot like riding a bike: there is an initial learning curve you have to go through, but once you've got it, you'll only need to revisit it every so often to brush up on your techniques.

You may want to practice your techniques on a patient friend, family member or colleague. If you don't have any of those available, you can always practice on a mirror. Rehearse what you'll say and how

Before diving into this book, you'll definitely want to thoroughly go through the Steps to Verbal Kung Fu for Freelancers section.

you'll say it. If you've ever watched Japanese martial arts movies you'll notice how effortlessly the fighters block, kick, punch and dodge — it's almost like they don't need to think about it at all. You can develop that same quick reflex "*when it's real*" through repetition.

Use Your Own Words, Not Mine

Bruce Lee had difficulty adapting to one martial arts style because he didn't want to be confined to just one way of doing things. Instead, he came up with his own free flowing style called Jeet Kune Do.

In that same spirit, use the phrases and responses in this book as a guide rather than a rule. If you find a better way to address a client than what I have, you should use it. The responses found in this resource are only a guide in helping you develop your own style.

Like Bruce Lee, you need to find what feels comfortable for you.

Have Patience

You wouldn't expect to be a black belt in your first week of martial arts, so give yourself some time to learn this. If you practice on a regular basis, you will soon become a master.

How This Resource is Organized

The core of this resource is focused on looking at the specific things clients claim, ask or demand that you do for them (I've included over 100 of the most common and frustrating for freelancers, they're called *verbal choke holds*). These choke holds are organized by category for easy access, you'll also find a handy index in the back of the book for quick reference.

Orange you glad you got through that section? You not find the master funny? Take your new orange belt and go!

RA

SECTION III:
The Steps to Verbal Kung Fu for Freelancers

"Remember that when you meet your antagonist, to do everything in a mild agreeable manner. Let your courage be keen, but, at the same time, as polished as your sword."

— Richard Brinsley Sheridan, 1751-1816, Anglo-Irish Dramatist

The Steps to Verbal Kung Fu for Freelancers

1. Avoid rushing in — let the client speak

Have you ever felt when you're talking to someone that they really weren't listening to you but are just waiting for their turn to talk? It's frustrating. So, even if you feel your client is absolutely crazy, you still want to offer them the courtesy of listening to them thoroughly before responding. If your client perceives that you are listening to her / him, this will go a long way in getting things moving in the right direction.

2. Remain calm and professional

It's challenging to remain calm on the inside and on the outside when you feel a client is blatantly trying to take advantage of the situation, but it's essential.

Suspend judgment, avoid jumping to conclusions, and keep in mind that you are seeing things from only **your own** perspective. You'll also want to be wary of the tone and speed of your voice. You can **drastically improve** a tough or tense situation by merely slowing down how fast you talk!

Next, be sure to use a gentle, non-threatening tone — it has a wonderful way of calming the situation and making the client more receptive to what you have to say.

Remember that non-verbal communication is much more telling than verbal (like 2 or 3X more), so be wary of your gestures, body

Never forget the power of silence, that massively disconcerting pause which goes on and on and may at last induce an opponent to babble and backtrack nervously.

— Lance Morrow

language, posture, facial expressions and eye contact with your client. Slowing your non-verbal communication is also a good way to improve a tense situation — keep your movements unhurried & precise.

Avoid accusing your clients at all costs, even if you know they are wrong or out of line. Remember, your goal in this is to gain cooperation and an understanding, not prove a point.

Lastly, even in a city of several million people, it's amazing how fast things get around. People love to talk, especially about conflict or a bad experience, so it's in your best interest to remain professional at all times. I know this is easier said than done, but letting a client get to you has a way of biting you in the butt if you handle it poorly.

3. Verbalize that you heard your client and understand her / him

Everyone wants to know they've been heard and understood, so this is a critical step. After listening to your client, pause for a moment and then you may respond back with, *"If I heard you correctly..."* You might try, *"Just to make sure I am clear, you are asking for..."*, or even, *"So you're saying..."* You can use whatever feels most comfortable to you; the point is if you can quickly summarize and repeat what a client has said to you it shows them that you listened and understand them. Try summarizing what your client said in your own words.

While this technique is helpful in dealing with clients, be wary of overusing it. You won't need or want to summarize every single thing you client says; if you do you'll come across sounding contrived and insincere.

4. Empathize

Once you've shown the client that you've heard and understood them, you can take this one step further and empathize with them. To empathize with someone is to identify with and understand someone else's situation, feelings, and motives. In this step, you might say, *"I understand why you might feel that way..."*, *"That's a good suggestion..."*, or *"A lot of my clients have asked for that..."*

Remember that seeing someone's point of view doesn't make them right, less aggressive, less demanding or less manipulative, it just means you can see things from their point of view.

5. Redirect the client and provide a reason why this is a fair solution

To this point you've listened, been polite and verbalized you understand. Now it's your turn to articulate your position/solution.

You won't need to go into a long explanation here. In fact, you won't want to. One or two very quick points are often all you'll need. The real trick to this working is to be confident, professional and provide a clear direction/solution for your client to consider.

Clients can often be like lions: if they sense weakness they'll pounce, so avoid being wishy-washy! Deliver your solution with succinctness and poise (if you are meeting in person with your client, maintain eye contact).

You can have unbelievable success on this step if your reasoning can include how this will benefit your client as well as you. For example, if a client wants you to charge them per project rather than per hour, you might respond with, "*I've had a lot of clients feel that way before they worked with me, but after they saw how much money they could save by electing to be billed hourly, they all made the switch.*"

6. Ask politely if your solution is agreeable and stand your ground

Most of the time, if you're in the right, and if you've been polite you'll have a good chance of your client seeing your point of view and going along with your solution.

The aim of argument, or of discussion, should not be victory, but progress.

— Joseph Joubert
1754-1824, French Moralist

To help lead your clients to agree with your proposed solution, you'll want to add one of these agreement questions right after you've proposed your solution:

- Does that sound fair to you?
- Would you be open to that?
- Will that work for you?

You'll always want to add a question like this at the end of your solution because it makes your client "feel" like she/he is in control...in reality you are in control of the situation! (*You'll quickly see how this works when you get to the verbal choke hold section*).

After you've delivered your agreement question, just sit there. It's crucial that you sit quietly and calmly so you give your client ample time to answer. Avoid fidgeting, looking around, tapping your pencil — just sit there confidently and wait for an answer.

Keep in mind that clients will often try to stall you just to see if you meant what you said. If your client doesn't answer, continue to sit there. If they don't respond, try, "*Sorry, about that, I asked if you would be open to that; I was just waiting for you to answer. Do you need more time or do you have an answer for me?*"

NOTE:

There are going to be times when your client will not respond to your solution. While most situations can be amicably worked out — not all of them can. If your client objects to your solution, walk them through your thought process again, varying things a bit and see if you come out with a different result. Keep in mind that sometimes a client will be insistent on getting her / his way no matter what you say.

If you've tried the *Verbal Kung Fu for Freelancers* approach and your client isn't responsive, you'll next want to try to compromise. For example, a client may demand you to drive all the way out to her office, you may try to comprise and meet somewhere in the middle.

If compromise fails (in some rare cases) you have to decide if it's worth it to just do what they ask or walk away. This can often be a big decision so buy yourself some time by saying, "*Well this is an important decision, I'd like some time to think it over. Would it be fair if I got back to you tomorrow afternoon?*"

Ah, you have passed another section — excellent. Wear your new green belt with humility and without envy.

防

SECTION IV:
Clients and Their Tactics: What They Want and How They Manipulate You

"Who digs a pit for others will fall in themselves."
— German Proverb

Clients and Their Tactics: What They Want and How They Manipulate You

Clients are looking to get you to:

- Lower your prices
- Offer them a discount
- Allow them to slide on paying you on time
- Barter for services instead of payment
- Give them free services
- Give them priority service before any of your other clients
- Allow them to stall on a project

Whatever their objective, the client is trying to get more out of you than they agreed on. This could be more value, more service, more time or more attention. Depending on what's happening in their life, you may find that one client is looking to get you to comply with a number of these at one time.

Recognize that **almost all** clients are frugal; they want to get as much of a deal as they can. Being frugal isn't bad; getting a good value is something everyone wants, but it's your job to decide what is acceptable and what isn't — when a client is being frugal versus when they are being demanding or manipulative.

You'll find the "give & take" compromise approach can be quite effective. For example, offering your loyal clients a few extra perks might make good business sense. If you have a client dropping $2000 with you every month and they are asking to get priority service over many of

> *Most quarrels amplify a misunderstanding.*
>
> — Andre Gide 1869-1951, French Author

your other clients, you might want to consider it! Managing clients effectively isn't about caving in to their requests, nor is it about taking a rigid approach with them. It's about negotiating, compromising and engaging in a collaborative effort.

You'll find that your client relationships will go a lot better if you are able to bend a little rather than break.

However, there are some clients that habitually try to squeeze everything they possibly can out of a freelancer or vendor. They'll continually try to take advantage until they get what they want — you either stand up to them (using *Verbal Kung Fu for Freelancers*) or you fire them. Hopefully through this book you'll learn to work with them, just understand that some clients can't be reasoned with. You'll want to determine which aspects you'll be willing to negotiate with your clients and which ones you won't.

Client Tactics

1. Guilt: making you feel sorry for them
2. Bullying: testing your boundaries; seeing what they can get away with. "*I want this*", "*I need this*"
3. Getting other people involved (friends, so called experts, designers etc.): "*Well, my friend said _____*"
4. Yelling, cursing, bad behavior
5. Pleading ignorance: "*I didn't know...*"
6. Withholding money for services
7. Promising things without any real intent to deliver
8. "Consistent history" strategy: "*We never had to do or to pay this before, so we shouldn't have to now.*"
9. Comparing themselves to other clients: they remind you that they are good clients to work with because they are nice, give you a lot of work, allow you more turn around time, etc.

You'll find that the tactics a client uses are a function of her / his personality. An aggressive, type A person might resort to bad behavior or bullying tactics.

Others will try less forceful tactics like pleading that they didn't know, or trying to make you feel guilty to get what they want.

This doesn't mean that one of your clients won't try 1, 3 or all of these tactics on you. I've had one client try 4-5 of these tactics in a span of a few weeks — you never know quite what clients will try! What clients try on you isn't important; how you react to their tactics is.

No, you won't need to memorize the above list; just become familiar with the more common ways that clients will try to manipulate the situation to work in their favor. Over time you'll become familiar with certain tactics clients will use to manipulate you — you'll be able to recognize them the moment the client tries to use one! Finally, this isn't a conclusive list, so you may even discover a few tactics clients tried on you that weren't listed.

Purple looks better on belt than on body as bruise — please accept your purple belt and get ready to train for your black belt!

MH

SECTION V:
Client Demands and Verbal Choke Holds:
Overcoming Them Using Verbal Kung Fu for Freelancers

"When you argue with your inferiors, you convince them of only one thing: they are as clever as you."

— Irving Layton, Canadian Poet

Important Notes Before You Begin Your Training

Your black belt awaits, my student, but before you make your way through these sections, you'll notice:

- Each example has a description below it that describes what your client might REALLY be saying. This should be taken as an experienced and educated guess rather than a hard, cold fact — if I could completely help you read your client's minds, I would have marked the price of the book higher! Use what I have as a guide, but trust your own intuition.

- In going through the *Verbal Choke Hold* section (the real meat of the book), you'll notice some of the text is in a lighter color and in a different font - this was done intentionally to make it stand out. This is to indicate a variable or contingency that will vary according to your specific situation.

  For example if you read, *"I'll be able to get this to you by Friday of this week"*, you should substitute **Friday of this week** for what is appropriate for you and your situation — which might be **Thursday of next week**.

- A few of the *verbal choke holds* in this section are similar to each other; this was actually done intentionally to provide you with a couple of different ways to address the client.

- After you go through a response to a *verbal choke hold*, you may come up with a better way of addressing the client than what I have. Not only do I support you doing this, I encourage you — remember, these shouldn't serve as flash card responses you memorize but guides to help you develop your own responses that feel and sound natural to you.

  If you've got a more comfortable way of responding to the client — do it!

Client Demands and Verbal Choke Holds:
Bringing Up Past Designers

While this section refers specifically to designers, it's applicable to all forms of freelancing and contracting. All students are welcome to proceed!

My past designer gave us the raw, master digital files...

Client is REALLY saying this to you, "I want you to give me the raw master files."

You: I've not had a chance to sit down and talk with your past designer so I am not sure what went into their methodology. I do know that the vast majority of true graphic design professionals in my industry don't give away their master digital files.

Client: Well I had one that did.

You: Many professionals do offer clients the ability to purchase the files at a reasonable rate. However, their agreement and mine indicate that you as the client will receive the finished flattened artwork. You will have the ability to take this artwork to virtually any printer and have it reproduced; you just wouldn't be able to make significant changes to it.

OPTIONAL:

You: Most of my clients didn't want or need the master files. They preferred that I handle all of their fixes and revisions rather than worry about them. Would it be easier if I just made the fixes for you?

You: There have been some rare instances when the client did request the files, in which case I offered them the low, low price of $500 - $1000, which is extremely reasonable considering the rest of the industry charges as much as $2000 - $5000. If you are interested in securing these files, I would offer the same arrangement to you. Is that something you'd want to take advantage of?

My past designer did that for us for free.

You: Thank you for sharing that. (You could just say this and sit there... the client is baiting you to defend yourself, and you don't have to.)

OR, *if they persist:*

You: Thank you for sharing that. I am not sure how that relates to me though... I've never met the designer you've worked with in the past so I don't know how they bill their clients. Do you charge your customers for your time, effort and expense?

Client: Yes, but sometimes I offer free services or products.

You: In some cases I do as well, but just like you, I am running a business and I deserve to be paid fairly for my time and expertise. Is that fair to feel that way?

The other designer we worked with did it for 25% less than you.

You: You'll find that like every other service professional, designers charge according to their skills, experience, talent, time and host of other variables, so it's tricky to fairly compare one price to another. How do you react when your customers say this to you?

Client: I tell them that you get what you pay for.

You: I don't know the designer you mentioned but I am sure he or she priced their time and services according to what they and their clients thought they were worth, just as I know what my time and expertise are worth. I've priced this work out myself with other design firms, and for the expertise and time I am providing, this is a great value.

My past designer was able to get the work turned around faster.

Client is REALLY saying this to you, "You're taking too much time getting my work back to me. You need to work faster."

You: I appreciate your honesty, but there might be more here than meets the eye when it comes to turnaround times. For example, I know some designers are able to turn projects out faster because they aren't as in demand, so the one or two clients they work for get fast service.

I am not sure if that was the case or not, but the way I've been able to build my business is to schedule clients in as soon as possible and make certain that I am not rushing projects out the door. Would you want me to rush a project out the door, or make sure I invest the time to make sure it's terrific?

Client: No, I'd rather you not just push it out the door.

You: It's important to me that I design something for you that you feel great about, and that brings about the results you want. Is that worth me taking an extra day or two rather than rushing something out?

Why do I have to pay you for our initial meeting when other designers don't charge?

Client is REALLY saying this to you, "You should give me this meeting for free. I don't understand why I have to pay for your time initially. I don't value your time."

You: I don't know the other designers you're specifically speaking of, so I couldn't answer for them. I do know that some designers value their time and need to account for it, while others don't. I also know that some designers build the costs of these meetings and their time into the price of the project. Can you see how designers might do this?

Client: I suppose so, but I just don't like the idea of having to pay for something like this.

You: It's like a car salesperson that builds undercoating into the price of the car — the client pays for it whether they know it or not. I have found, as most of my clients have, that if I charge up front and fairly with all of my time it's easy to account for costs and in the end it's more cost effective.

Would you rather have upfront pricing and just pay for the time that you need or have the costs hidden from you and secretly built into the project?

It used to take my other designer just 15 hours to get this done (This statement is usually made when you are billing hourly).

Client is REALLY saying this to you, "I don't trust how much you're billing me. I feel like you are charging me too much. You're taking too long to finish the project"

You: I can appreciate you saying that. I am concerned with completing your project in a timely and cost-effective manner for you. At the same time, it's imperative that I design something that I know you'll not only feel good about, but that's going to help you bring in more business and customers. If I'm taking a little more time to do this, wouldn't it be worth it to you?

OR...

You: I can appreciate you saying that. I am just as concerned with the quality of the project I am delivering as I am with the speed in which I deliver it.

I know the average designer will take up to 15 hours to complete a project like this. I could get the project done in the same amount of time as you're suggesting, but I want to make sure I don't purposely rush it out and end up with something that's not going to be as unique and effective as you would like it to be.

RA

It's always exciting to be working with a new client, bringing new business in - just remember that even mousetrap provides free cheese...at a price.

Client Demands and Verbal Choke Holds:
Payments and Pricing

If you charge hourly does that mean I am basically giving you an open-ended check book?

Client is REALLY saying this to you, "I am afraid you're going to charge me more than I expected. I am afraid I am going to be stuck with a huge bill and I won't be able to do anything about it."

You: That's a very good question. A lot of my clients were initially a bit nervous about this until they heard how we do things. Being billed at an hourly rate ensures that you only pay for the time and services that you want, rather than being hit with a *"one size fits all"* invoice.

Let's say a designer typically spends 20 hours on projects just like yours. If you are able to help him or her get it done in 1/2 the time you still end up paying the full amount. Does that sound fair? Shouldn't you just pay for what you use?

OPTIONAL:
Explain how you help them control costs. I would recommend this...

You: I know you might be thinking, "Well, how do I know how much this will cost me?" Right?

Client: Yes, that's definitely a concern of mine.

You: Well projects like this do typically take me between 5-8 hours. That would mean your investment will be somewhere between $250 - $400. Will that be comfortable for you?

Client: That could probably work.

You: I will help you determine how you can get that number down to the lower end of the scale. That's right, I will help you learn how to save money on this project. Does that sound like something you'd be open to?

Client: Of course.

You: I will also let you know when we hit certain time benchmarks, such as 5 hours and 10 hours, so you'll know where your costs are. I will also keep you informed of when I feel we're ahead of time / budget and when we need to pick things up a little.

If we do run into a situation where we're going to noticeably go over my estimate, I will give you as much notice as possible, and I'll let you know why we're over our time budget. I'll make a recommendation as to how we can get back on track and allow you to decide what you want us to do from there. Does that make sense to you? Does that sound fair?

Try to give people the benefit of the doubt; even if you don't feel they've earned it.

Why do you charge by project rather than other designers that charge hourly?

Client is REALLY saying this to you, "Am I going to get a fair deal if I hire you? Can you help me see why the way you charge will give me a better deal?"

You: That's an insightful question, and I am glad you've asked it. Clients have always expressed to me that they wanted the ability to control their costs — to know exactly how much they have to budget for a specific project. I know a lot of other designers charge an hourly fee, but you're never certain exactly how much your invoice is going to be, right?

Client: No, I guess I wouldn't. I would have to take their word for it.

You: I would guess it would be a bit unnerving giving a contractor you've never worked with before an open-ended checkbook, wouldn't it? That's why I bill clients on a per project basis, so they can control their costs. Does that sound like the way you'd want to work with someone you've never worked with before?

Why is your hourly rate more than other designers I've talked to?

Client is REALLY saying this to you, "Help me understand why I should pay more for you."

You: That's a good question; I hear it a lot. I am assuming you're not the most inexpensive vendor in your industry, so have your customers ever asked you the same question? How do you respond to them?

Client: Often I tell them that they get what they pay for, or that we just provide a much better service or product.

You: Exactly. But in addition to the difference in value, there's another way to look at this, and you may warn your customers of this as well: shopping on hourly rate alone versus what you get for your money can be misleading. Would you agree?

Client: Absolutely.

You: Let's say for example that you charge $10 an hour and your competition charges $8. What your customers may not know is that you can do the job in half the time as your competitor, or that your work is that much better than your competition.

Also, the competitor charges for the interview meeting, travel time, teleconferences, and even just thinking about your project.

My design company only charges for actual design time, in-person consultations, and half time for teleconferences lasting over 30 minutes. So do you see how a freelancer could easily hide costs from you?

Client: I suppose you're right.

You: It may look like a bargain but in the end they get you to pay more. What you might consider doing is shopping on value rather than hourly rate — what exactly will you get from your investment. Do you see how this might be a better way to go to ensure you get the best value for your money?

MH

How much for a *web site?*

Client is REALLY saying this to you, "I haven't done my homework and I have no idea what I am doing. I am just browsing today. I have my defenses up right now."

You: I don't know. I work with clients individually, and one size fits NONE is our core philosophy. I'll be happy to meet with you, learn more about your business and objectives and give you a tight quote based on your actual needs for the project.

Client: Well, I just want a price quote.

You: You can easily get price quotes by going on to the Internet and typing in *"designer pricing"*, but you're never sure if that's a fair price or not. Is this what you want or do you want to be assured you're receiving an accurate, fair price for the work you want to have done?

You used to charge me $800, but now you're charging me $1000.

Client is REALLY saying this to you, "Explain the price increase, and why I have to pay it."

You: Yes, you are right about this. My costs have gone up a little in this area, but I've kept costs as low as I can for everyone. I do know that other designers are charging as much as $1250 - $3000, so I am trying to keep costs as competitive as possible.

OR:

You: Yes, you are correct. If you remember the last time I did your quick web updates in less than 10 minutes because they were minimal and this time I'll be doing extensive changes to not only the text on your web site but also your layout. This is the difference between the two costs.
Does that make sense?

I thought that business cards were included in the price.

Client is REALLY saying this to you, "Why do I have to pay for this? This is an unexpected and unwelcome surprise. Please explain to me why this isn't included in the price."

You: Sorry about the confusion on that. I've never had free business cards as part of the package, so could you tell me where the miscommunication came from?

Client: Well, I thought we talked about it one time, or I thought you might have emailed that to me.

You: I think you'll find in our proposal that it spells this out on page 5. Let me know if I can help clarify things further.

OR:

You: Sorry about the confusion. No, it's not included in the price. So I can make sure to avoid any confusion in the future, would you let me know why you thought that?

In working with clients; follow the number one rule in boxing: "Keep your hands up and protect yourself at all times."

I can't afford to pay for that, but I need it done.

Client is REALLY saying this to you, "I am unwilling to pay for it. Please give me a price break."

You: Well, there are always other options out there. Is this something that you're going to be using to build and grow your business? Do you understand that you can always pay less money, but you may get a lot less return on your investment? Are you willing to accept a lower return on your money and your time?

Client: I guess I know that but I can't afford it right now.

You: I know that cash flow can be a challenge for almost all business owners. That's why I don't require clients to pay all the balance up front, and I do allow clients to pay in easy installments. If you have credit power, why not consider financing this project by putting the balance on a credit card?

OR:

You: When you say you don't have enough money for it, is it because the project will never be funded, or is it just bad timing? If you have a credit or debit card, you have credit power and you can afford this. We can set up extended, stretch payments to make things easier. Would that be helpful?

OR:

You: I'd love the opportunity to work with you, and I feel we can design something you're really going to be happy with. How else can I make this affordable for you?

I'd like to work with you, but can you do something about the price?

Client is REALLY saying this to you, "Can I get this any cheaper? Will I be able to get a better deal if I can haggle?"

You: That's great — I'd like to work with you as well. Based on our conversations, I am confident that we're going to enjoy working with each other and you'll receive a project that you'll love.

This is a great price for the project we've mapped out together, but I can certainly make some modifications to the project scope in order to accommodate your budget. What items or tasks should we remove from the project scope that aren't quite as important?

Client: They are all kind of important, I guess... Why do you ask?

You: By removing some bells and whistles we'll be able to get the value of the project more in line with your budget. We can always address these later when there are more funds available (if the client doesn't know, make suggestions for him or her).

You know, if we hold off on doing the **trifold brochure** until a later time, that will save you between $750 - $1500. This will get us pretty close to where you need to be with the budget. Does this sound like it will work for you?

It's important to know that some people, **no matter what the cost is, will always want to haggle with you.** It's in their blood. Whether they are or aren't in this case doesn't matter — just tie the budget amount to the work that you're doing.

They want more, they pay more; they want to pay less, they get less.

In this little equation, the client is expecting you to leave value and the project scope constant and change price. What I've done here is to change value and the project scope, which affects price.

If you help us with this project we'll be able to bring in some revenue and pay you some money.

Client is REALLY saying this to you, "We don't have money or we're not willing to risk spending money. Rather than paying you what you are asking for, we want you to take on the risk of lowering your rate now and hope you'll get paid more if the company and project are successful."

You: Sorry to hear things are tough, it seems to be tough for everyone right now.

OPTION A — *You don't gamble:*

You: I know this can be a difficult position but I need to be paid fairly for my time, just as you do with your business. Right?

Client: Sure.

You: You don't provide goods and services to your clients in the hopes that you're going to get paid, do you? Can you in good conscience ask me to do so?

Client: I suppose not, I am just trying to make this work.

You: I can appreciate that, but unlike the big corporations, I am a small business and making sure I am paid fairly and promptly for my services is critical. I get paid or I don't eat.

OPTION B — *You gamble:*

You: If you have any credit power, we can make arrangements today whereby you can make payments on the balance. All you need to do is put a credit card on file and we'll be all set. Do you have good credit?

Client: Yes (*Note: Most clients will avoid saying "No". No one wants to admit they have bad credit*).

You: Great, In order to make this work, I will need to draw up another proposal that has the new terms on it. We'll need to agree on specific dates and amounts you're going to be paying me, and you'll agree to pay for any and all fees associated for collecting payments that are not on time.

I would like to help you out because times are a little tough; this is how we can make that happen. If this is agreeable, we'll move forward. If it isn't we'll have to put your project on hold until funds become available.

If you can give us a price break on this project, we'll pay you extra on the next.

Client is REALLY saying this to you, "I am unable or unwilling to pay you what you want. I wonder if I can tempt you into the project by promising work later?"

You: If you were in my position, would that sound like a good deal to you?

Client: Maybe; it depends on the client.

You: Exactly. But since you and I just met, it's a big risk on my part, wouldn't you agree?

If I were to accept your terms that you'll pay me more on the next, would you be comfortable putting that in writing?

Client: I am not sure. I guess so.

You: Okay, if you agree to do another project with me in writing for twice my normal rate, you've got a deal.

One last question though, what if something unforeseen comes up on your end and there doesn't happen to be a next project, where would that leave me?

Diplomacy is the art of letting someone have your way.

— Daniele Vare

My budget is $500, firm.

You: I congratulate you on setting a budget. I've worked with a lot of clients that haven't established one. It shows you've done some thinking about where this is headed, and that's good.

Client: Well... thank you (your client will be a little surprised by your response — that's good!).

You: Knowing what we have to work with will help me plot a specific course of action based on your needs and the funds that are currently available. I can certainly work within that budget. What we'll be able to accomplish in that budget is designing the look and feel for your company with the logo and the business cards.

What I might suggest is using this project as stage 1, whereby we get things rolling for you. When this project starts producing some results, you'll have some more funds to invest, either in this project or another one.

In the above example, see how a negative was turned into a positive? Take the route of coming along side the client and talk about what "we" have to work with rather than forming an adversarial relationship.
Sensei say, "*Handshake always better than punch to face.*"

I am not sure what my budget is.

Client is REALLY saying this to you, "I am afraid to tell you what I can or want to spend. I am afraid that if I tell you, you will raise your prices on me. I don't trust you enough to be honest with you."

You: Thank you for being honest about that. I do know that it takes some time and effort to devise a budget. At the same time, it's going to be difficult to help you if I don't know what kind of a budget you're working with.

Client: (Your client will probably just nod at this point; there isn't much they can say and they most likely won't disagree with your logic.)

CP

You: This would be like visiting a car dealership and saying I want a car but I don't know what will fit into my price range — you could be shown Pintos or Porsches.

In order for you to get the help you are looking for, you'll want to be able to provide some idea of what price range will be comfortable for you at this time. Does that make sense?

Client: Yeah, I suppose so, but I am still not sure what my budget is (this may be true, or the client is not being honest with you).

You: What we might find helpful is finding out if you're thinking:

1. Whatever it takes, this has to succeed
2. Within reason; I want good results but a fair price
3. Tight budget; I just want something put together so I have something
4. No funding for the project at this time; I need to work a trade or another arrangement

Which one of these options best describes the situation you are in? The project you're looking to have done typically will run clients between $500 - $750.

Assuming you're going to be thrilled with the design I come up with, would that be comfortable for you? If that's not comfortable, what range would be?

Is there another way we can work this out?

Client is REALLY saying this to you, "I am unwilling or unable to pay you what you're asking. I'll see if you are willing to negotiate with me."

You: What other way do you mean? Do you mean, I'll do the work for you and you'll pay me with something other than money?

Client: I don't know... Can we work some sort of a deal or a trade?

You: Well, I appreciate the offer but the way I run my business, as do other graphic design professionals, is to design excellent work and charge a fair price for it. Do you offer trades to people in your business?

Client: Yes. Sometimes they don't work out but sometimes they do.

You: I'd love to see if we can find a way to work together, but my mortgage, car payment and utility bills won't take trade or other arrangements, so money seems to be the best option. If cash flow is currently a bit of a challenge, you can easily put the balance on a credit card. I'll even allow you to pay over time rather than all at once if that will help you. Does that sound fair?

Is there something we can do about the price?

Client is REALLY saying this to you, "I am unwilling or unable to pay you what you're asking. I'll see if you are willing to negotiate with me."

You: If I were able to adjust that price quite a bit, would it suggest to you that my original price was inflated and too high?

Client: I suppose so.

You: For what I am going to be doing for you — designing a first-class business card, logo identity and stationery package — I am charging a very fair price. What is the absolute most important thing we have to accomplish with this project?

Client: I'd say getting a logo and a business card.

You: Why don't we concentrate our efforts in this first phase on accomplishing that goal? This will reduce the price of the project, and you'll still be able accomplish your main goals. How does that sound? We can address the stationery package in phase 2 of the project.

OR:

You: To include all of these services, we need to charge just $1000; it's a fantastic value for this package of services. I can reduce the price to make it a little more in line with your budget. Which item(s) can I remove from the list to reduce your price?

The goal here is to NOT reduce price or haggle, but to start taking bells and whistles away from the project in order to reduce price. Sensei say, *"Never reduce price without reducing the value of the project."*

I am looking for someone to partner with on this project. You'll get a portion of the profits!

Client is REALLY saying this to you, "I don't have any money, or I am unwilling to spend any money. I am going to see if I can sucker someone to buy into my idea rather than pay for a designer. I will try to convince you my idea is a great one, even though I don't have a lot of faith in it."

You: What does that mean? Does that mean you don't have any funds to pay a designer right now?

Client: Cash is a little low now, but this is a terrific idea that anyone would love to get in on at the ground floor. I am offering a great opportunity for you to make some big money on my idea.

You: It sounds like you have a lot of passion for this idea, but what happens if for some reason the business model doesn't work? Does that mean I won't get paid? It sounds like I am going to be bearing all of the risk, and if it doesn't work out I'll be out of luck. Does that sound fair?

OR:

You: I can appreciate that you are looking for a partner. The way I've built my business by doing a great job for clients and charging a fair price for my services — I am in the graphic design business, not the restaurant business. The way you and I can work together is that I work for you — you get great design, and you pay me fairly for my time. You may be able to find a less talented or more inexperienced designer to accept your idea but in my experience, most talented professional designers will pass.

Client: $@*&! (*There really isn't much the client is going to say; if he or she continues to argue with you, or just packs up and leaves, they never intended to pay you to begin with — and they never will*).

NOTE: If you do decide to gamble on the client, make sure you use your leverage. You should be getting paid MUCH MORE than you would normally because you are bearing a lot of the risk.

Make sure you negotiate something in writing that will heavily reward you if the idea takes off. You should have an attorney draw up and / or look over the agreement. If the client doesn't want your attorney to get involved, don't do business with her / him.

A gentle answer turns away wrath, but a harsh word stirs up anger.
— **Proverbs 15:1**

I'd like to work with you, but I've received bids from other designers and they are less expensive.

Client is REALLY saying this to you, "I'd like to work with you, but I want to see how desperate you are to have my business. Let's play chicken and see who blinks first."

You: You're right. You can always spend less money on a less expensive option, but are you willing to accept a smaller return on your investment? Are you willing to accept that you might not be getting the results you're looking for with a cheaper option?

Client: I don't mind paying some money for this; I just don't want to get ripped off.

You: Are you the least expensive vendor in your industry (*they will say "no"*)? Then what would you tell prospective clients when they tell you, "*I can get it cheaper?*"

Client: No, we're not the cheapest. We offer good service and products at a reasonable price. If a customer tells me this I might tell them that they'll get what they pay for or I might just tell them to go ahead and go somewhere else.

You: Most businesses owners that offer a valuable service would say the same thing, including me. If you do not want to compete on price to get customers, does it make sense to hire a design company that solely competes on price to get their customers? Wouldn't it make more sense to hire a designer that can compete on value rather than price, since you'll want to do the same?

Client: I suppose I never thought of it that way.

You: If a designer could really help your business grow, do you think they'd offer the lowest price out there? If I could provide your business with outstanding design, service and results, wouldn't you guess that I would always be in demand and I'd be charging a premium price for my expertise? I'd be a fool if I didn't. Inexpensive or discount rate artists are cheap for a reason — they're not very good.

Have you had other projects designed by professional designers? How did they turn out? In terms of dollars and cents, what kind of a result did you get? Did you think it was worth the time and money you put into it? What did the designer create for you, and what was the budget associated with it?

Client: I've worked with other designers before; it's turned out okay.

You: If you don't mind me asking, why aren't you working with one of them on this project?

Why should I pay you to design my web site when I can just get a template or go through an automated online system?

Client is REALLY saying this to you, "I can get this cheaper and see no need to pay more for the same thing unless you can convince me otherwise."

You: You know, I am asked that question a lot. I've had the chance to see some of the templates the web site factories have pumped out, and some of them aren't too bad. What you may want to keep in mind though are the two biggest complaints business owners have shared with me over the years in having a web site developed with one of these templates: the web site just sits on the internet and doesn't do anything for their business. They were grossly disappointed at the lack of guidance, direction and service the template company provided.

Client: Yeah, but you are charging three times more than what I can get it for.

You: Let's first back up a bit and identify your goal for the web site. I am guessing that since you are in business, your goal is to attract customers through the web site. Correct?

Client: Sure.

You: Of course... Your goal for the web site is bring in results, but that's not the goal of the template vendors. Their goal is to sell you a decent-looking web site, take you through a quick, regimented process and send you on your way. Will you save a couple of bucks? Sure, but you're going to be doing most of the work and you'll feel like a car on an assembly line.

My objectives in working with you ARE to help you bring in more customers, to help you develop a site that actually looks good — and works — as well as to guide you through the process and allow you to focus on running your business rather than worrying about the web site. Do you see the difference?

Client: I suppose so.

You: Looking to save money when possible is always a good idea — I know; I run a small business too. Going the template route is a great option if the business owner is strapped for cash, has a lot of time and patience and isn't all that concerned about results. Would that describe where you are today, or are you looking for something more out of your investment?

The client is doing one of two things here: he or she is either looking for you to sell them on your services because they might be interested, or they just want you to have to defend your prices so they can feel better about going with a cheaper option. The challenge is knowing which. Sensei say, *"Trust your inner voice when making judgments about clients; if your voice says nothing then ask a knowledgeable colleague."*

Client Demands and Verbal Choke Holds:
Afraid of Commitment

I am having several freelancers come in to interview. I'd like you to come in too. Are you available?

Client is REALLY saying this to you, "I want to show you that I don't see a big difference between you and other designers. A lot of designers want to work with me. I am in demand."

Some introductory questions you might ask:

- What are you going to be looking for in these interviews?
- What materials will I need to bring to help you decide if I am the right fit for you?
- I appreciate you cutting some time out of your day to meet with me. What is it about what I've said or what you know of me that makes you feel I might be a good fit for you?
- What criteria are you using to make a decision on who will be the right fit for you?
- If you don't mind me asking, how any freelancers will be interviewing for this project?

NOTE: This one's tricky: on one hand you want to make sure you don't throw away a good opportunity. On the other hand, you don't want to be part of a parade of freelancers going in and out of an office having no real chance of being hired. This really depends on how much you want to work with the client and how good you feel your chances are of being hired.

Some clients shuttle freelancers in and out of their office like cattle, just so they can feel they've made a good decision, so be aware of that. Even though they like only one or two designers, they may bring in half a dozen of them just to convince themselves that they've made a wise decision.

Because the freelancers are traveling to their office, it doesn't cost them much time or money, so it's no big deal — for them.

OPTION A — If you feel there's a good chance you'll be hired and you're willing to gamble:

You: I'd be happy to come in. I can appreciate that you want to make the right decision for you and your company.

Let me ask you though, when I've completed the meeting with you, is there any reason why you won't be able to tell me if you are going to hire me?

If not, when will you be making your decision?

Client: Probably not right away; I'd like to see what everyone can offer me first.

You: (Decision time — is it worth it?)

OPTION B — You're not sure if the client is even interested, and you want to test them to find out:

You: I'd like the opportunity to work with you, but it sounds like you're still in the shopping stage of your decision.

Client: Yes, I am still looking around to see what's out there.

You: My schedule over the next few of days is tight, which is a mark of a busy, in demand freelancer. I'd be happy to teleconference with you now or a specific time later, find out what you're looking for and help you decide if I am the right fit for you.

If after our teleconference you feel like I would be a solid fit for you, we can set up an in-person meeting. Does that sound fair?

Can you send me a proposal and let me think it over?

Client is REALLY saying this to you, "Please spend some time working up a proposal; I'll use it as a benchmark to compare you against others. If I think you'll give me the best value I will hire you."

You: I would be happy to. If I had everything over to you by Thursday at 3:00 PM would that work for you?

Client: That would be fine, get it over to me as soon as possible.

You: Great, I'll have the proposal over to you by Thursday at 3:00 PM. I'll check back with you the next day, Friday at 12:00 Noon to see what you've decided. Does that sound okay?

Client: I may need more time.

You: No problem. I want to make sure you have ample time to make the right decision for you. How about I call you on Monday the 8th at 11:30 AM?

I will be able to answer any last minute questions and we can talk about how you want to move forward. Fair enough?

Make sure that if you send a proposal they commit to a specific timeframe to give you a definitive decision.

RA

I'd like to set up another meeting with you to talk about how you can help me.

Client is REALLY saying this to you, "I am not ready to hire you, and I'd like to see if you can provide me with more value that I don't have to pay for. I'd like you to give me some more ideas for free."

You: Just so I am clear, do you need more information to make an informed decision, or would you like me to come in as a consultant and provide specific recommendations as to where you should go from here? What specifically are you looking to accomplish in this meeting?

Client: I am pretty sure I am going to hire you; I just want to ask you a few more questions and make sure it's the right fit for me.

OPTION A — Client wants more information:

You: Is there something else specifically that you need to hear or see that will provide you with enough information to make a decision? I want to make sure you feel comfortable and confident hiring me. How can I do this and make good use of your time and mine?

OPTION B — Client wants answers to specific challenges they have:

You: I'd be happy to sit down with you and help you choose the colors and options for your business cards. As you know, there's never a charge for our first meeting. I would estimate the second meeting will take between 60-90 minutes, which will run you about $75. What time would be good this week to schedule this?

OR — A little more forceful:

You: I do appreciate the offer, and I'd enjoy meeting with you. The way that I work with clients is that I don't charge for our initial meeting since we're going over general concepts such as thoughts and ideas about your business, goals and project requirements. I do, however, charge clients a very reasonable fee of just $75 for a comprehensive 60-90 minute meeting, where we look into providing specific solutions for their situation.

Client: What suggestions can you give me about my brand?

You: From our meeting, you will walk away being clear on your options, knowing what marketing collateral to choose, learning to not use the color red in your logo, etc. Would it be worth it for you to have me come in and sit down with you as your consultant and help you come up with some specific solutions?

You're showing clients the difference between providing **general FAQ's that clients have versus specific answers to their design challenges.** General questions are no problem, but when you feel the client is just "*pumping you*" for information, you need to let them know that specific questions can certainly be answered but they need to pay you for your time and expertise.

I'd just like to set up a meeting where I can learn about you and get some ideas on where to go with my business.

Client is REALLY saying this to you, "I am not ready to hire you, and I'd like to see if you can provide me with more value that I don't have to pay for. I'd like you to give me some more ideas for free."

NOTE: This is a tricky one because there are potential clients that legitimately want to meet you and get some general ideas on where to go with their business.

There is another group of people though, that have no real interest in hiring you, and in fact many of them might not be able to hire you even if they wanted. Instead, their goal is to pump you for as much information as they can.

These people need help and aren't sure where to start, so their goal is to set up meetings with designers and glean information off of them.

These people aren't bad — desperate and misguided maybe — but not bad. They are, however, bad news for a freelance designer who doesn't get paid unless he or she gets hired.

I've come up with a way to uncover if these people are legitimately interested in you or not.

Here are some quick questions you can ask the client to size them up:

- I appreciate that you are willing to take the time to meet with me. How do you see that I am going to be able to help you?
- Do you have a specific project or projects in mind that you want designed? How do you think these projects will help your company?
- What is it that you hope to gain from meeting with me?
- Have you ever worked with a designer before?
- Have you taken a moment to view my online portfolio? What about it suggested to you that I might be worth meeting with?
- Do you have a budget in mind when it comes to this project?
- When do you need to have this project done?
- Have you shopped around and looked at other design options?
- What criteria are you looking for in hiring the right designer for you?

Try to give people the benefit of the doubt, but based on how they answer the questions above, if your gut tells you that they are just pumping you for information, you can say:

You: It sounds like you're still in the information gathering stage, which is no problem. Instead of taking up your time before you've had a chance to look around, I would suggest contacting a couple of other designers to get a feel for what's out there.

I'll be happy to check back with you in a few days to find out if you feel that I might be a good fit for you to hire. What phone number will I be able to reach you at?

RA

Mock up something, and if I like it I'll pay you.

Client is REALLY saying this to you, "I am not sure I'll like what you create, so I'll see if you'll do something before I pay you, or I am looking to get free ideas."

You: I am certainly looking forward to showing you what I can do for you; I think I'll be able to capture something you're really going to like. How I work with clients is that I provide them the opportunity to evaluate all of my work in my portfolio and ask any questions that they would like. They can even look at or call my references.

Based on this information, if they feel I am a good fit for them, they pay me a deposit and I begin work on their project. I even offer them a guarantee that they'll like what I've come up with. Does that make sense?

OR:

You: I could throw something together quickly, but if I take the time to create something for you, I want it to be something you'll really like. This takes a lot more time and effort than simply putting together a mock-up and hoping you'll like it.

Client: I guess so; I just wanted to see what you might do for me.

You: I want to make good use of my time and yours. I think I'd do a great job with this project, and if you feel I'll be a good fit for you, what would be stopping you from hiring me?

OR — This is a little more forceful:

You: I'd be happy to work something up for you. What happens if it's not exactly what you're looking for? Will you still pay me?

Client: No, I'd pay if you if I liked it though.

You: What would you say if someone contacted you, asked you to do work on the premise that you might get paid? Would you do the work? If not, why would you ask me?

Why don't you design something, and if we like it we'll hire you?

Client is REALLY saying this to you, "I am not sure I'll like what you create, so I'll see if you'll do something before I pay you, or I am looking to get free ideas."

You: I can see why that might be important to you, especially if you've been burned by a designer before. But if you go to the grocery store, they don't let you take home food without paying for it. Why should I be any different?

Client: I am not sure, but the grocery store has products and you sell a service.

You: That may be, but we both have inventory: the grocery store's inventory is their products. As a service provider, my inventory is my time. If I do the work on this project and you elect not to pay me, I'll be out as much as 5-7 hours with nothing to show for it.

If the situation were reversed, would that sound fair to you?

Client: Probably not. Still, what if we don't like what you've created?

You: That's a great question. There's always a small risk when working with new people. In order to put you a little more at ease, I've brought a number of my past designs so you can get an idea of what I'll be able to do for you. I also have several testimonials from satisfied clients just like you who were thrilled to work with me.

I am not sure now if we even need this project. Maybe we shouldn't move forward.

Client is REALLY saying this to you, "I am either frustrated, confused or a combination of both. I need someone to step in and give me some consulting advice."

You: I understand you may have questions and or concerns. Let me reassure you: that's normal. Here are some questions you might ask yourself to help make a decision:

- How much would it help you?

- Do you think you could raise your prices?
- How do you think your clients, prospects and competition will react?

- Do you think this will help you attract new clients? How many?

- What got you thinking that you should do this project? There's obviously something you're wanting to change or improve in your business. What could it be?

- What happens if you decide to do nothing? Will things go back to the way they were? Will they get worse?

- How long have you invested time in thinking about or talking about having this project completed?

- Do you feel not having this project completed at this point is negatively impacting your business? In what ways?

NOTE: These are all quick questions designed to get your potential client to realize that it's in his or her best interests to move forward with the project. It causes them to step back from the fear and look at what's going on from a more rational standpoint.
They may decide they don't need the project, but it's unlikely.

You'll meet with my assistant and he or she will give me the details about you and the project later.

Client is REALLY saying this to you, "I am too busy to meet with you, working with you is not high enough on my priority list."

You: It's been my experience that both the client and I benefit tremendously if we meet face to face. This will give you the chance to learn how well we'll communicate together, and give you the peace of mind knowing I am a good fit for you — which I've learned is so important to clients. Additionally, things inevitably seem to get lost in translation when communicating through an intermediary. Would you think it would be worth your time to take 45-60 minutes to meet me?

Client: I'd like to, but I just don't have the time.

You: I can understand that you're busy, and I appreciate your honesty. I am flexible with my schedule, so if time is a bit of a challenge for you, just provide me with 3-4 times you'll be available to meet over the next week and I'll make one of them work for us. We can also schedule a teleconference at your convenience as well. Would that make it easier?

OR — This one's a bit more forceful:

You: I'd be happy to meet with your company, but since your assistant won't have the authority to make the decision to hire me or not, I'd much rather meet with you as well. I'd love the chance to sit down with you. Is there a reason why we can't all meet?

Avoid meeting with assistants, receptionists or anyone else but the person that has the authority to make the decision to go ahead with the project.

If you're meeting with people that can't hire you as their freelancer, you're probably wasting your time. Try to only agree to meetings when you know the decision makers will be present. Sensei say, "No decision-maker; no meeting."

Drop off your mock-ups or sketches and we'll decide later if we want to hire you.

Client is REALLY saying this to you, "I am too busy to meet with you. I want you to commit to working with me, but I don't want to have to commit to working with you just now."

You: If I drop off the sketches to your office Thursday at either 9:00 AM or 3:00 PM, will you have time to sit down and look at them?

Client: No, but I have some time at lunch. I could do it then.

You: That sounds fine. I'll be happy to sit down with you and go over what I've prepared for you. Assuming that you like the sketches, is there anything else keeping you from moving forward with the project?

CP

Why don't you look at what I have and what my competitors offer, and then give me some ideas?

Client is REALLY saying this to you, "Give me a free analysis and free ideas and maybe, just maybe, I will hire you."

You: I'd be happy to provide you with a very quick analysis of what's going on with your design and offer some general ideas. If you would like me to provide something more extensive, I am able to provide you with a comprehensive review in a couple of hours of time. It won't run you any more than $125 for the time I'll invest. Would you like me to do that?

Client: No, don't spend a lot of time on it (*your client will probably back off here, because they most likely wanted you to do it for free*).

You: No problem. Again, I'll be happy to provide you with some quick thoughts I have. If you'd like something more specific and in-depth, I'll want to invest some time in it to make sure I am providing you with first-rate information.

NOTE: Notice I placed a value on doing market research when the client did not. The client does not place any value on this, and that's why he or she asks you to do it for free. I still told the client I would help, but if they wanted a comprehensive analysis, they'd have to pay for it.

If you don't assign a monetary value to the time and expertise that you bring to the table, don't expect your client to tell you that you should charge for it.

Let me talk to my business partner before *we move forward with a commitment to hire you.*

Client is REALLY saying this to you, "You haven't totally sold me yet. I need more time to either talk to someone else, gather more information or look at other options."

You: That's no problem. I want to make sure you're comfortable moving forward. What additional questions or concerns do you have that I can address for you?

Client: No, I think I should just check with my partner first (*this may be true, or the client may be stalling*).

You: What will you and your partner discuss? How will you make your decision to move forward or not? When would you like me to check back with you and see what you've decided? (*Feel free to use any or all of these.*)

NOTE: Notice I first tried to get the client to move forward without stalling. If that doesn't work, try to find out what concerns he or she has.

Finally, avoid allowing the client to say, "*We'll just call you when we know.*" Instead, take the initiative and make sure you have control of the process by offering to call them back.

Before I hire you for this project, I'd like to call some of your past clients and talk to them about you.

Client is REALLY saying this to you, "I am worried or not convinced that you are the right designer for my project. I am not totally sold on hiring you yet."

You: I can understand why it would be important for you to get a good feel for what I can do for clients. If I were in your position, I'd want to get some reassurance, too. I want to respect the privacy of my clients, but I do have a number of testimonials you can review. Would you like me to show them to you?

Client: Yes, that would be helpful.

OR:

You: I can understand why it would be important for you to get a good feel for what I can do for clients. While I do have some impressive testimonials for everyone to review, I want to respect the privacy of my clients. I would have to check if this is okay with them before you contact them.

Client: Sure, I can appreciate that.

You: If you haven't had a chance to look through my testimonials, might I suggest looking at them first, and if you still feel you need to contact some of my clients we can discuss it. Will that work for you?

I noticed you haven't been in business that long.

Client is REALLY saying this to you, "I am worried that you are inexperienced or that you won't last in business."

You: You're right, I've been doing graphic design for over 3 years, and I decided earlier this year to turn my talents and passion into a full-time freelance career. As you can see, I've got some significant experience under my belt with the projects I have in my portfolio. Wouldn't you agree?

Client: I am not sure. You do seem to have a number of projects though.

You: I know in some industries, the length of time someone's been in business is important, but I've found that the most critical requirements clients are looking for are: attitude, strength of portfolio and reliability.

Would you agree those things are more important than how long I've been in business?

I just need you to work up some prices for me and I'll decide later.

(This is typically a phone call or email from a prospective client.)

Client is REALLY saying this to you, "I don't want to commit to anyone right now because I am shopping for the best deal. I am gathering information and I want you to help me make a decision based on price."

You: Are you looking for someone to help you today or are you just gathering prices? Would you like someone to help you understand your options and make recommendations on what you can do next based on your needs?

Client: I do want to sit down with someone but I think right now I need to get prices.

You: Price checking is certainly something you'll want to do. What I've found is that business owners are either ready to move forward with a project and they just need to find the right person, or they are unsure if they can or want to move forward with the project. Which camp do you think you're in right now?

Client: Oh, I think we'll be moving ahead with this. I just need to stay within our budget.

You: I can appreciate that. Since no one has unlimited resources, all of my clients need me to work within their budget. Is it worth an hour of your time to see if I can meet your needs, or are you content with gathering prices?

OR — if an email is sent, try this:

You: Thanks for your email. I'd be happy to talk to you about your vision, expectations and goals!

If you are just shopping around for prices, you can Google *"logo design"* and get prices ranging from a few hundred dollars to a couple thousand. From being in the business for a decade, here are the top 3 complaints I have heard from business owners when dealing with inexpensive designers:

1. *"The designer didn't bring any ideas to the project. They just used my ideas."*

2. *"I paid the designer a bunch of money, but it didn't help me build my business whatsoever."*

3. *"The project was done late, I didn't like it and the designer told me there's nothing I can do."*

In hiring the right designer for you, my friendly advice would be:

- Hire a designer who's going to care about you and your business. Look for someone who will bring fresh ideas on how to get the most out of your project

- Only work with designers that have a 100% money back guarantee.

- Make sure your designer has verifiable, compelling testimonials.

Business owners bring me on board when they want a **truly unique design that sets them apart from their competition.** If you'd like to have someone like that on your team, give me a call. I'd love to talk with you!

I always get 3-5 price quotes before making a decision (or I am still looking around at other options). When I've made up my mind I'll let you know.

Client is REALLY saying this to you, "I don't want to commit to anyone right now because I am shopping for the best deal. I am gathering information and I want you to help me make a decision based on price."

You: Shopping around is always a good idea. Is there anything else you need to see or to know in order to feel good about your decision to work with me?

Client: Nope, I think I have everything I need for now.

You: If you don't mind me asking...

- Are you going to be basing your decision on who to hire solely on price?

- What other criteria will you look at in making your decision?

- Would you like help in deciding who might be the best fit for you?

- Finally, when would you like me to check back with you and see what you decided?

I'd like to see more examples than what you have on your web site. Can I see more?

Client is REALLY saying this to you, "The examples on your web site were okay, but they didn't convince me you were the right designer for this project. Do you have better designs or more applicable designs elsewhere? I am not feeling confident about hiring you based on what I have seen."

You: I'd be glad to help you. What is it you were hoping to see that you didn't see on the web site? Is there something specific that you are looking for that I might be able to show you?

What else are you hoping to see or hear that's going to help you make a comfortable decision on whether I am the right fit for you?

Client: Not really, I was just hoping you had something else that was similar to what my company offers.

You: While I may or may not have designed something specific to your business industry in the past, can you see that I've designed successful projects across a wide variety of industries?

Would you have any reason to doubt that I could do it for you as well?

NOTE: What is really happening here is that the client isn't convinced yet that you are the right choice. He or she is asking you to provide more evidence to prove you're the right fit.

Sure, there is a chance you've got some recent work that's not on the web site, but most people would assume that your best work would be featured. It's important to get to the root of what their issue is, and it's almost never that the client needs to see more artwork.

In your never-ending quest to slay the monsters of this world, be careful not to become one...don't let bad clients turn you into an angry person.

MH

I am interested in using your services, but I am going to have to put it on hold for the time being. I have some money coming in and as that happens, I will probably use your services down the road.

Client is REALLY saying this to you, "I don't have any money. I want to look around and see who else I can hire. I don't want to say "no" right now, so I'll tell you I'll 'probably' use you."

You: Thank you for the kind words. I'd like to work with you as well. I know estimating when money will come in can be tricky — are you thinking a few weeks or a few months?

Client: I am not sure, just when it comes in.

You: If you don't think it will be that long; I can always help you out by restructuring the payment plan to fit your needs. Will this help you? You mentioned this project was a priority, and you were anxious to move as quickly as possible, so let me know how I can help you and we'll find a way to get this rolling for you.

OR — This one's a bit direct so be careful in using it:

You: Thanks for the kind words. I thought I'd be a good fit for working with you as well. I know a few variables have to fall into place in order to find the right designer: cost, availability, personality, etc., and I know sometimes the funds you need just aren't there. Is this a case where money all of a sudden got tight or is it just not a good fit for you?

CP

Client does not respond at all after you've sent over a proposal. Even after following up, the client doesn't return phone calls or emails.

Client is REALLY saying this to you, "I am too busy now. I am not interested now. This isn't a priority now. Or I have found someone else, and I just don't want to tell you 'no'."

NOTE: While this isn't something a client verbally says to you, like the other entries in this book, the client is sending a clear message to you, and I wanted to take a moment to address it.

If a client has asked you to send a proposal to him or her, agreed they would get back to you by a certain date, and they've just not done it, you have a bit of a challenge on your hands.

There is a danger of jumping to the conclusion that the client is not interested in you or just blowing you off. You might feel angry or upset about this, but I would caution you against assuming the worst. If in fact the client has a reasonable explanation why they didn't get back to you, you're going to feel like a jerk for accusing them of blowing you off, and you'll certainly lose the business.

Suspend judgment until you've learned all of the facts. The client may have blown you off, but it's in your best interest to give them the benefit of the doubt. No one likes being in limbo and not knowing what happened to a client. **I have found that a often the client didn't mean any harm; they just decided to go in another direction, or they didn't have enough money to do the project.**

They might feel embarrassed or guilty that they took up your time. Some clients just can't deliver bad news like, "I appreciate your time but we're not going to hire you." The key to avoid being in limbo and making these people feel at ease is to address this before you agree to send the proposal over to them. Try the following:

You: I am happy to send this proposal over to you; I can have it over by this Thursday at 1:00. Will that be okay? Would this Friday at 3:00 give you enough time to think things over and give me your decision?

Client: That's fine.

You: Great, would you do me one favor as you're looking through the document?

Client: Sure, what is it?

You: My goal here is to help you make the right decision for you and your company. I know that a lot of things, such as budget, time lines and design styles, need to line up for a designer to be the right fit for someone. I would just ask that by this Friday at 3:00 you let me know if this is going to be a good fit for you or not. If you decide to go another direction, there'll be no hard feelings.

I am excited about the opportunity to work with you, and I think I'd be a good fit. Let me know whatever you decide, and whether I should be getting ready to help you make some great improvements to your company's design. Would you be able to do that for me?

I'd like to get together and just talk about this project a little bit. When would be a good time?

Client is REALLY saying this to you, "I need some help and advice and I either don't want to pay for it, or I am home you'll meet with me without charging me anything."

You: I'd be happy to meet with you so I have a clear idea of what you're trying to accomplish. Let me ask you — what is

Being right half the time beats being half-right all the time.

— Malcolm S. Forbes
1919-1990, American
Publisher, Businessman

the purpose of the meeting? Are you just kicking ideas around, still deciding if you want to move forward, or are you ready to proceed with the project and just need some time frames and budgets?

Client: Well, we're pretty sure we're going to move forward. We just wanted to gather some more ideas.

You: Sure, that's always a good idea. How soon are we moving ahead with the project, and what's the budget for the project?

Based on the client's answer (or lack thereof), you may want to consider this final response, especially for clients that you feel might be taking advantage of you:

You: Again, I'd be happy to meet with you. It sounds like you'll be looking for me to provide some creative ideas and direction. For these initial brainstorming sessions, I do offer a discounted rate to make things more affordable. For a one hour session we'll be looking at just $75. When would you like to schedule a time?

NOTE: The client asked to meet for a brainstorming session on the latest project they were kicking around — sounds innocent enough, but if you're not vigilant, **clients will often be happy to chew up a lot of your time and not pay you**. Your goal is to find out if they're seriously looking to move forward, or if they are fishing for free creative ideas from you.

In defense of the client, sometimes things change in business and as a business owner you're often forced to reconsider or pull the plug on a project.

Your goal as a freelancer is to try to get an accurate picture up front on the situation before committing your time.

You wouldn't dive into the pool unless you knew how deep the water was, and you wouldn't drive on tires that you haven't checked the air pressure on (at least I hope not). The same idea can be applied in this situation.

I just found out that my grandfather is very ill and I need to pay for plane tickets back home. We need to put the project on hold until I've had a chance to sort things out here and find enough money to pay you.

You: So sorry to hear this John. It's always tough when a family member gets sick suddenly like this; it's happened in my family as well.

What might be best, if you're open to it, is to have you give me a call when the right time to get your business rolling. Drop me a line and we'll get you rescheduled at a later date — I know you have a lot on your plate now.

Client: Yeah.

You: If I haven't heard from you in a while, and if you don't mind I'd like to follow up with you in a while and see how you're doing, would it be okay if I contacted you in a few weeks and see how things are going? Would that be okay with you?

Client: Sure that'd be fine.

Is there an outside chance the client could be lying to you about a sick, dying or dead relative? Yes, it is possible, albeit very unlikely.

What you will want to do here is to be compassionate, but professional. There's a real danger of you getting sucked into all of the drama, and you want to avoid it at all costs.

Sensei say, *"Unless you're also a licensed grief or family therapist, stick to creative freelancing and avoid the drama."*

I am not *Jewish*, I am just *spiritual.* Is that going to be a problem?

Client is REALLY saying this to you, "I can potentially see a problem working with you because your beliefs about religion are different than mine. Convince me otherwise."

You: I would guess that I have clients with all different religious affiliations. Of course, my goal is to help small business people and my focus is web design so the topic of religion doesn't come up much. I care, respect and work hard for all of my clients regardless race, color, or creed. Does that sound okay with you?

Client: I suppose so...

You: I'd welcome the chance to work with you. Do you see this as being a challenge?

NOTE: Seems like an obscure example to include in this chapter, but it's happened to me twice in my career already.

Client Demands and Verbal Choke Holds:
Empty Promises

We know a lot of people that we can refer to you. Give us a deal and we'll refer all of our friends to you.

Client is REALLY saying this to you, "I don't have a lot of money or I don't want to pay a lot of money. Maybe I can get it cheaper if I bait the designer with referrals."

You: Exposure is fantastic, but it's something I've never counted on in building my business. How I've done as well as I have is by doing a fantastic job for each client, being paid fairly for my time and then moving on to the next client.

Out of curiosity, what makes you certain that I would be a good fit to work with your friends? What if I provide you the discount and on the off chance that it happens that your friends don't decide to work with me - it's not such a great deal for me, is it?

Client: Uhh, I suppose not...
(*Watch the look on your client's face — they'll be baffled you asked this question*).

You: I'd welcome the chance to work with you, it feels like we're a good fit — I am confident I'll earn your trust and maybe

It takes two flints to make a fire.

— Louisa May Alcott, 1832-1888, American Author

even a few referrals down the line, but I'd rather they not be part of the negotiation for the project but something that I've earned because you really liked the work I did and genuinely know people that I can help, does that sound reasonable?

After we get rolling with this project, I'll be sending you tons of business.

Client is REALLY saying this to you, "I might get better service, value or attention if I promise more business in the future."

You: That sounds good; thank you. Who do you know in your networking circle that would be a good fit?

Client: Well, I am not sure at the moment, but I can probably think of some people later.

You: Great, why do you think I would be a good fit for some of these people you know? (This will test to see if they really have someone in mind, or if they're just making it up.)

Client: I've liked the work you've done and I think they may need help too.

You: Hey, that sounds good. My focus right now is designing a project that you're going to feel great about and that's going to get you more business. After I've completed your project and only after you've indicated it was a success, I'll specifically let you know what type of clients I am looking for and ask you who you know that might be a good referral fit based on those criteria.

NOTE: You might just have a generous client that will want to share you with all of his or her friends — that's terrific! However, you may find that a client will try to use this as a phony incentive to get more out of you. In reality they don't know anyone they can refer to you. By asking specifically who they are thinking about and why they think they are a good fit, you essentially call their bluff.

After you find out their answer, thank them, but stress that your focus is helping them get a great result on their project. This shows the client that these types of "in the future" incentives really don't do anything for you.

I am going to be telling everyone I know about your talents and skills.

Client is REALLY saying this to you, "Treat me right and I'll help you make lots of money."

NOTE: This one is similar to, "*After we get rolling with this project, I'll be sending you tons of business.*" But it's slightly more vague, so I decided to provide a different response. I've heard this a few times in my career, but I still don't know quite what it means.

Near as I can tell, it's the client's way of telling you that you are appreciated. Often times the client means well but ends up telling no one about you.

Their heart is in the right place but they aren't that motivated to take action. Whether they are trying to get extra value/attention or they legitimately want to promote you, **I've found the more people insist they're going to promote you — the less likely they actually will**.

You: That's nice, thank you. Do you think you'll know of some people that might be a good fit for me? Tell you what, once we get your project wrapped up for you and you're happy with the results, we'll sit down and map out a referral program that will reward you for sending people my direction. How does that sound?

Client: Uh, okay.
(*Your client will be surprised you handled their comment like this*).

OPTIONAL — If you want to have fun with the client, call their bluff and try this:

You: Well that's nice, thank you. What will you tell them, and who will you tell?

Client: Uh, I'll just tell them you're good (*cue shocked look, again*).

You: Great. You will be telling them nice things right?
Who specifically will you tell about me and why?

No matter how true or not true it is, some clients think they spread joy to all - they might be spreading something, but it's often not joy!

MH

Keep doing good work for me, and I am going to keep you busy for a long time.

Client is REALLY saying this to you, "You'll want to take care of me and treat me right, because I am going to be one of your best clients."

You: I'd like that. Right now I'll focus on doing one project at a time and continuing to build value for you. If I continue to bring in good results for you, you'll probably want to keep on working with me. I've really enjoyed working with you; you're easy to get along with and we always seem to create something fresh and unique. I'll be looking forward to seeing what we can do next.

NOTE: Your client may be sincere about continuing to work with you, but this is a good sign. Sometimes you may find that a client will try to use this as a phony incentive to get more out of you on the current project.

In reality, they don't know if they are going to have the money or will want to work with you. If you take this as a nice compliment rather than a promise to work with you, you will be fine.

By responding with words of kindness back to the client and emphasizing what you need to do for them right now, you show your client that you are focused on their immediate concerns and not your own future gains.

I've been freelancing for about 10 years, and in that time my best clients NEVER said something like this when we first met.

Silence is not always tact, but it is tact that is golden, not silence.

— Samuel Butler, 1612-1680, British Poet, Satirist

Client Demands and Verbal Choke Holds:
Contracts

The contract is too long. Can you just send me a summary?

Client is REALLY saying this to you, "I don't feel like reading this. It's too complicated. Can you make it easier for me to do business with you?"

You: Yes, I know it can be a bit long but the proposal I sent over is designed to eliminate misunderstandings and keep us on track. I know it takes a few minutes to go through, but it lays the foundation for how we're going to get your project done. The good news is that most of my proposals are similar in nature, so when you've gone through the first one, you'll be able to go through subsequent ones quickly.

OR:

You: Sure, I can attach a quick summary that hits the highlights of the rest of the proposal. I know it's not anyone's favorite thing to do, but taking a few minutes to go through the proposal I have is definitely worth your time. Perhaps you can read the summary page now and go through the rest of the proposal when you have more time; just be aware that you would be responsible for what's included in the full proposal. Clients have never had an issue with my proposals in the past, but I just wanted to make you aware of this.

A lean compromise is better than a fat lawsuit.

— **George Herbert, 1593-1632, British Metaphysical Poet**

I can get the contract over to you by the end of next week. Can you get started working today?

You: If it's all the same to you, I'd rather make sure we get the proposal turned in and out of the way before I begin — it saves the time and hassle of trying to track it down later when our focus is really on designing a great web site for you. Does that make sense?

Client: Yes, but we'll probably have to wait until later next week to get started?

You: I understand. I'd like to get started quickly with your project as well, so if you'd like to get started today we can do a couple of things: you can fax the proposal over, you can drop it off, you can send a courier or you could even scan it and email it over. I have several options you can choose from, so we can get your project started ASAP. Which one of them sounds best for you today?

Client: I'll get my assistant to fax it over later today.

You: Great, I'll keep my eye out for it. Once I receive the completed proposal, I'll get that tucked away and get your project officially off the ground.

I can't get to a fax machine, or my fax machine is broken. Can I just verbally agree to the contract?

You: That's okay. Tell you what, I can wait until you do have access to a fax machine. If that won't work you can always have the proposal mailed over. If you'd like to get started today you can send a courier or you can even scan the proposal and email it to me. Sounds like we're both ready to get started; What option is going to be best for you?

Client: I'd like to get started now.

You: Sounds fine; I'd like to start right away as well. Which of these options is going to be best for you?

NOTE: Focus your response on what you can do rather than what you can't. Empathize with the client in that you want to get started too, and you're willing to provide easy, logical ways that you can get started.

Notice I've avoided talking about my policies or rules about contracts. It's difficult to tell if the client has a legitimate excuse here or not, but the fact of the matter is that if it's that important for the client to have you start ASAP, **they WILL find a way to get the signed proposal over to you.**

We've never signed a contract before. We don't normally sign contracts. Why do we need to sign a contract if we trust each other?

Client is REALLY saying this to you, "There is something about your contract, or contracts I've had in the past, that I am not comfortable with."

You: Have you ever heard the phrase, "An ounce of prevention is worth a pound of cure?" I know proposals can be a pain, but they clearly define the job parameters and responsibilities so there is no miscommunication down the line.

Pause here and let the client respond or acknowledge what you've just said.

You: This proposal specifically outlines what you receive from working with me and when you receive it, safeguarding both parties from misunderstandings. Doesn't that sound like something that you'd want?

Client: I suppose so, but I don't know why I have to sign it.

You: You wouldn't accept a job from a company without clearly defining the terms, so why would you object to this? Is there anything specifically in the proposal that you find unfair?

Notice I avoided calling it a contract — *"proposal"* is a much less threatening word to a client. Sensei say, *"It's a proposal when you're signing a client to a project; it's a contract if that client decides not to pay."*

I haven't had time to go through your contract.

Client is REALLY saying this to you, "I am dealing with other things right now, and starting this project isn't a huge priority at the moment."

You: That's okay; I know most of my clients have a lot on their plate. Will you be able to commit to getting to it by this Wednesday the 23rd?

Client: That would be fine.

You: I've found that one key element to having a successful project is to keep things moving forward and maintaining momentum. I'm dedicated to designing your project on time and on budget, but I'll need your help to do this.

A spoonful of honey will catch more flies than a gallon of vinegar.

— Benjamin Franklin, 1706-1790, American Scientist, Publisher, Diplomat

If you can get through the proposal by **Wednesday the 23rd** that will keep us moving forward, and we'll avoid any delays.

NOTE: Be careful in this example that the client isn't just testing you to see if you really have a legitimate contract AND that you're going to enforce it. Over the years I had a number of clients try everything in the book to avoid signing a contract — stand your ground and do not let them get away with such tactics.

Client Demands and Verbal Choke Holds:
Project Turnaround Times

I know we've been a little slow getting the changes back to you, but you'll still be able to complete the project by next Tuesday — right?

Client is REALLY saying this to you, "I know I haven't kept up my end of the bargain, but I still need you to come through for me. Can you bail me out?"

You: I do know things come up, so it's no big deal. We got a little off track which might cause some challenges. The changes came in about 3 days late, so at the moment we'll be just a bit behind schedule.

Assuming we don't have any further snags or delays, we're looking at a delivery date of next Friday instead of next Tuesday. I am going to do my best to keep our original schedule, but we might be just a little bit late.

OR:

You: Sure, I can get that done for you. I am going to have to work a lot faster but I think I can help you out here. I do want to let you know that in the future, if you are delayed in getting things back, I understand, but I might not be able to work my magic and bail you out of a jam. Does that make sense?

OPTIONAL — This is a bit more forceful. Use it if your client is insistent that you meet the original deadline, but they were blatantly late and you can still bail them out without killing yourself:

You: I will do my best to get this back to you on time, but it's important that both you and I keep things moving along. Since the web site revisions were 3 days late, I'll need to work 3-5 hours of overtime in the evening or on the weekend to make up for the delay.

I can do this but it will **increase the cost of the project by $75-$125.** Is that something you'll want me to schedule in, or is the slight delay going to be okay?

NOTE: You're going to want to make sure that your contract states that getting the project done on time is a joint venture and that if the client is late with their responsibilities it can, and often will delay the project's delivery.

Clients unintentionally do this frequently to designers. They often don't get critical aspects of the project back to the designer to keep things rolling. Consequently, the designer is left waiting for changes, feedback, materials, etc.

Even though the client was late in holding up their end of the agreement, they hope the designer will bail them out.

In addition to indicating this in your agreement, make sure you send a follow up communication email or call the client and say, "*I will need that list of web site revisions from you soon to keep the project on time. I know that's important to you, so I'll need it by 2:00 this Wednesday at the latest. If I receive it after that, it's going to delay the project. I just wanted to give you a heads up so you can make adjustments if your deadline is still important.*"

It's always nice to bail a client out every once in a while — just be careful you don't teach them bad habits. They can and will take advantage of you when they are late getting something back to you on time.

... Everyone should be quick to listen, slow to speak and slow to become angry.
— **James 1:19**

I need you to get the project done early because I have *a trade show* coming up.

Client is REALLY saying this to you, "I may or may not be willing to pay a rush charge, but I want you to bump me ahead of all of your clients and projects if necessary."

NOTE: This scenario is set before the project actually gets started.

You: I should be able to accommodate that request. Based on workflow requirements, I can officially start your project on Tuesday. Should I lock that time slot in for you?

Client: That would be great.

You: All you need to do is place your deposit down today and that date won't change — that will be your spot. If you decide to hold off until later, that's okay but that will push the date back a little. Would it be better to lock in your date now?

OR:

You: I can do that for you, but understand that getting a project like this done on time will require both of us to commit to getting it done. In order to make this happen for you, I'll need the web site content as soon as possible, and all feedback returned within 24 hours. How early can you get these to me?

Client: I am guessing by Friday.

You: Great, I'll mark that down. If we can both agree that you'll be getting all of the materials to me by then we'll be in good shape. If you get delayed, just understand that it may affect our ability to get your project done when you need it. Just to make sure I am clear — you'll be able to get everything to me by Friday, correct?

NOTE: If you don't know exactly what you'll need and when you'll need it by, tell your client you will need a little time to organize this. Tell him or her that you will get back to them at a specific time later that day or the next. You'll probably want to specifically list out all of the things you'll need and the exact dates you'll need them by.

If the client needs to provide you with materials so you can get the project done, make sure you make the completion date and time contingent on her/him getting that stuff to you timely. All too often clients will submit content, graphics, feedback late and yet still expect you to be on time. Since they are involved in the project as well make sure they are accountable for getting it done as well.

That won't work. I need to have the project back to me by Friday at noon. Or... Why do I have to pay a rush charge?

Client is REALLY saying this to you, "Your workload doesn't determine when I get my project. I, as the client (and my schedule), decide."

You: I understand that deadlines are all part of the freelancing business; I try to accommodate everyone as much as I can. Most designers will take **up to two weeks** to complete this project. I typically can do it in **5-7 days**, which is pretty quick wouldn't you say?

Client: Yes, but I need it as quickly as you can get it to me.

You: I can get the project done for you **by Tuesday of next week**. If you still need the project done faster than that I might be able to help you out. I do offer special priority service for projects that need to be done in a hurry. I'll need to bump some clients from my schedule to make room for you, and I'll have to work overtime hours to get this done for you.

Client: That sounds good.

You: I can get it done for you by **Friday**. I do charge a priority rate for this service of **1 1/2 times** my regular competitive rate of **$75 per hour**. I'll be able to guarantee that your project will be done on time. Does that sound like something you'd like to move forward with, or do you want to stick with our original agreed upon due date?

You've always been able to get this to us in 3 days in the past, so I figured we'd be okay.

Client is REALLY saying this to you, "I didn't check with your schedule to see if this could be done. I assumed that you would be able to help me immediately, no matter how much you have on your plate."

You: If there was confusion there, I apologize. I avoid telling clients I will always be able to get their project done within a specific time frame because my workflow fluctuates quite a bit from week to week. In addition to completing your project, I have 2 others in front of it. To make things fair, I complete work on a first come, first serve basis, so completing your project might take me more or less time depending on my workload. Does that make sense?

Client: I guess, but when can you get my project back to me?

You: Based on my current workload, I should be able to get your project done by next Thursday. In the future why don't we agree ahead of time when your project will be completed so you'll know exactly when to expect it and we'll avoid any miscommunications?

How long will my brochure take? When can you have this back to me?

Client is REALLY saying this to you, "I have a rough idea how long this will take, but I want to see if you can meet my expectations."

You: I can have this back to you within three days of receiving your deposit and the content you want to use on the brochure.

NOTE: While this kung fu move looks like innocuous, it's extremely valuable. Clients always wanted me to give an exact date or time when I would be to get a project or mock-up back to them. The challenge was that they often played a big part in how much time I had to turn a project around.

For example, a client would ask me when they could see a version of their brochure. I would quickly respond back, *"By Friday of this* week." Unfortunately the client owed me content to put into the brochure, which they didn't get to me until the night before.

Since I committed to getting the brochure done on Friday, the client still held me to that, even though they were late getting me the content.

If you need the cooperation of the client or a third party, tell the client you'll be able to get whatever they need done in a specific time frame — say, 4 days — **after** you've received everything you need.

This way you'll never get boxed into meeting an unrealistic deadline when other people are holding you up because they haven't gotten things to you on time.

Sensei say,
"Hey, that's a
great looking
guy there!"

MH

I can fax you over some of the content. Is that okay?

Client is REALLY saying this to you, "I don't have this in a digital format. I either don't know it should be in an electronic file, or I don't want to type it."

You: Faxing is okay, but I'd really prefer that you email it. That way we'll know that all of the content is readable since it's digital...I've found that faxes don't typically come across okay.

Additionally, I will be able to use exactly what you have instead of worrying about whether I read and typed what you wanted correctly.

Client: I'll have to have someone type it up before I send it to you.

You: I understand. When it comes to coming up with great design, I am your guy, but I am not the fastest typist in the world. Additionally, I've found it much easier to avoid misinterpretation and typos if I just copy and paste exactly what you've sent me. I appreciate your willingness to have someone quickly type it up on your end and email it over. Thanks.

NOTE: Make sure you know the contact information of a couple typists that can help out if the client doesn't want to do it. This is an easy way to avoid having to do the typing, help your client out and make a few bucks by sending out a referral. It's a win, win, win!

OR — If you don't mind typing this up:

You: Sure, fax away. I've done a lot of typing for other clients as an added service; it saves them a load of time. It usually takes me about 10 minutes to type up a page, which will keep the costs below $150 for everything you'll need. Do you think it's worth it to go ahead and have me type it for you?

NOTE: Unwitting designers are often so eager to get the content that they forget that if it's faxed someone has to type it. If you find this happening to you frequently, you might consider addressing it in your contract as an added service that you to offer to clients at a specific cost per hour.

I have a CD with the materials you need on it. Should I drop it off, or can you swing by my office and pick it up?

Client is REALLY saying this to you, "I am offering a lot of ways to get this CD to you. This project is important to me."

NOTE: This one's especially for freelancers that work out of their home and prefer not to have clients coming in and out. At the same time, they want to avoid becoming their own courier service.

OPTION A — You want to meet the client somewhere that's more convenient than his or her office:

You: I am looking forward to receiving it so we can keep things moving. I will be out and about today running some errands and attending some client meetings. Can we go ahead and meet at the coffee shop on 44th and Frazier Avenue around 2:00?

OPTION B — You want the client or a courier to drop it off but you don't want to meet them there:

You: I am looking forward to receiving it so we can keep things moving. I will be out and about today running some errands and attending some client meetings. You could send a courier over to my place or even drop it off yourself. All you have to do is leave the CD under the door mat, and it should be fine. Will that work for you? If it does, about what time might you drop it off?

OPTION C — You don't want the client coming to your house and you don't have time to meet them. Instead you'll send your own courier:

You: I am looking forward to receiving it so we can keep things moving. I will be out and about today running some errands and attending some client meetings, but I have a courier that I frequently use in these types of situations. I can have them pick up the CD between 2:00 and 4:00 today. This will save you making a trip and me going crazy with my schedule. Will that work for you?

I am not sure what format these files are in, but I'll send you what I have.

Client is REALLY saying this to you, "I don't want to take the time to sort through the materials you need. I'd rather you go through it for me. I might be assuming there's no charge for this."

NOTE: This situation often occurs when the client isn't sure what they have to send you and they really don't want to know — they want you to sort it out.

Depending on your agreement, you might be obligated to do this, but for most designers, their project scope doesn't include rifling through the client's "stuff" to organize and make sense of it.

You certainly want to be helpful, but be careful about falling into this trap.

You: That sounds okay, but it might save us both some time if you take a couple of moments to check out what you have before you send it over.

If you present yourself as a doormat, clients will have no trouble walking on you.

Client: I am not sure what to look for. I would rather you take a look.

You: I can certainly look at it, but if you've looked it over before you send it over you'll be able to help me make sense of it a lot quicker, which will keep us moving forward much faster. Do you think that's a good course of action?

OR — If you want to be a bit more forceful, you might try the following:

You: Sure, I can look it over for you. It's a little outside of our project scope, but I can take a few minutes and see if I can put some order to what you have.

If I find that it's going to take me a while, I'll let you know how long I think it might take, and let you decide if you want to invest in having me do it. Does that sound okay?

MH

My original files are in Word and Excel. Can you work with them?

Client is REALLY saying this to you, "I am hoping these files will be worth something and that we won't have to redo everything."

You: Sure, I can give it a try. I know a lot of clients have files in these types of programs. They really aren't professional design programs, so it might take me some work to get what I need out of them and into what I'll be working with. Is that okay?

Client: I guess so. I am not sure we have another choice at this point.

You: I'd suggest sending the files over to me and letting me take a quick look before I commit to anything. Based on what I find, I'll let you know if we'll be able to do this easily or if it's something that's going to require me to invest some time.

This is a little outside the project scope in our agreement, but if it doesn't take me that long, I'll just throw it in as a freebie to you. When can you send the files over?

NOTE: This one looks innocent enough, but I know of designers that rue the day they responded to this question with, *"Sure, I can do it for you. No problem."* It can turn into a big problem.

It's always best to go in with a positive attitude. However, if you don't know what kind of files, software version, or platform the client is using, let the client know you'll look at what they have and then let them know what you can do.

We're going to need to put the project on hold for a while.

Client is REALLY saying this to you, "I don't want to do the project anymore, I can't do the project anymore, or I found someone else I want to do the project."

You: No problem, I understand things come up. Remember we agreed in the proposal that you would be making payments on June 1st, July 1st and August 1st, whether or not the project was on hold. When you're ready to resume the project there will be a 10% **rescheduling fee** to get you back on the schedule. Just call and we'll get things started again for you.

Client: Okay, but why will I have to pay a rescheduling fee?

You: Unlike stores that sell products, my inventory is my time. I strategically assign specific dates and times when I'll be working on a project like yours. This is how I manage my workflow and keep projects on time for clients. When a client pulls a project it creates a hole in my work flow.

When I resume their project, it causes me to rearrange my schedule to accommodate them and in some cases it forces me to work overtime.

NOTE: You don't have to assess the rescheduling fee, but I'd recommend putting it in your contract to discourage clients from putting you on hold.

I found a lot of these pictures on the Internet. Will you be able to incorporate them into the project?

Client is REALLY saying this to you, "I don't know about or don't want to pay for stock photography. I don't understand copyright infringement."

You: We might have a couple of challenges with this. We'll want to make sure the photos or images aren't copyrighted before we use them. If you found them while surfing on the Internet, there's a good chance they are.

Client: I didn't know that. Is it a problem?

You: If we incorporated them into the project, the rights holder could hold one or both of us liable, so we want to make certain we're aren't infringing on someone else's rights.

Also, the photos you pulled off the Internet were probably low resolution, which means that while the images look okay on the computer screen, they might look fuzzy or blurry when printed. We want to use only high resolution images for artwork that's being printed.

Client: What can we do about it?

You: My advice is that we look at what you've found and see if we can find some similar or even better images on an online stock photography web site.

I am just not sure which logo I want.

Client is REALLY saying this to you, "I am unsure which of your logos is the right fit for me. Help me choose; sell me on one of them."

You: Remember what we've talked about all along — do your best not to over think selecting a logo. This is where a lot of business owners tend to become overwhelmed, bogged down and lose a lot of time.

Based on our brainstorming about your business and your clients, I believe any one of these logos is going to work great for you. Selecting one of these logos over another isn't really going to affect sales for you, so we're really just looking at art and personal preference.

As we look at the examples I've created for you, I believe the three strongest logos I provided you are #2, #3 and #5.

Be sure to explain why each logo is a good fit.

You: While the other logos will definitely work for you, I believe you can't go wrong with any of these three. Which one do you think is the best fit for you?

Client: Well, I like #3, but I am still not sure.

You: I can see why you'd choose that one. I felt that particular logo might be a good fit because it does achieve the balance we talked about and still gives off a friendly vibe. I think it's a great fit with your personality and the customers we're hoping to attract for you.

Do you feel good about moving forward with it?

The key here is to sell your ideas and artwork. Remember that you're the expert; that's why the client hired you. The client most likely has no experience designing logos for a living so it's important that you take the lead from the beginning.

If going around and around on a revision merry-go-round is a challenge for you, you'll want to check out my **Creative Freelance Designer's Audio Success Series**. I cover this topic in great detail so you immediately take command of the situation rather than feel like you're being led by your client.

Client Demands and Verbal Choke Holds:
Approvals and Changes

I know we've gone through this several times, but I still have more changes for you to make.

Client is REALLY saying this to you, "I don't understand or don't care about how long you budgeted for this project. I feel that if I've paid you, I should get what I want, no matter how many changes I ask for."

You: I'd be happy to make the changes for you. I do want to let you know that we've gone a little beyond the project scope due to the number of changes you've requested.

Client: Okay, what does that mean?

You: What I can do is take a look at the changes you have here and see what we're looking at. If they are simple, I'll just go ahead and make them. If they are going to require a lot of time I'll give you a call and we'll talk about what we want to do. Are these the last changes you'll have on the project?

NOTE: The last question you should ask is, *"Are the last changes you'll have on the project."* This is a crucial question to ask in trying to make the client make a decision and commit to finishing the project.

If she/he indicates there may be more fixes you should tell them that it's in everyone's best interest to wait until all of the final fixes have been identified and then you'll talk them over. If you don't do this you'll often find yourself doing round after round of revisions.

Either through ignorance or greed, clients often feel like it's not a big deal to have you do keep making changes at their whim. You'll need to educate your client that while you do want to please them, you can't keep making change after change with no end in site. Tell her/him that there is no charge for the next 1-3 rounds, after that you can keep making changes but you'll have to account for your time.

I need you to make some "quick" updates to my web site.

Client is REALLY saying this to you, "I need some updates. I might agree to pay for them, but if you just give them to me for free I won't complain..I'll call them easy or quick so you'll feel guilty about charging a lot."

NOTE: This scenario assumes you are not currently working with the client, but you've done a project for them in the past.

You: Sure. Do you know specifically what changes you'll need?

Client: I think so. I need the address changed and I'd like our new toll free number on there. There might be some other ones too. How do we move forward with this?

You: Either we can specifically go over them on the phone or you can email them over to me. I'll let you know how much time it will take me and give you an approximate cost for the work. Usually, I can get changes like this done in about 24-48 hours. Does that sound okay?

NOTE: Clients always tend to underestimate how long their project/fixes/revisions will take; they either do this because of greed or ignorance. Either way, it's your responsibility to confidently but professionally educate your client on how long their work will require (and why if necessary).

Clients will always try to lower their bill however they can, so don't get too upset. Stay professional and stay calm.

Never communicate with a client when you're angry.

Even if you need to make a fake excuse to calm down, avoid engaging a client when you're ticked off.

Can we try out some other concepts before I approve this design?

Client is REALLY saying this to you, "I am not confident in my ability to make a decision. You haven't sold me on the design so I'd like to see if you can come up with something better. I may or may not be aware that this may extend the project scope."

You: We can certainly try a different angle but is there something specific about the current design that you'd like tweaked?

Client: I am not sure; I just want to see if you can come up with something else.

You: I understand and I want to let you know I am committed to making sure you're happy with what we come up with. Are we doing more designs because there's something specific you'd like to see changed, or are we just coming up with more designs for argument's sake?

Client: I sort of like what we have; I just want to see what else you can create.

You: I am guessing it will take me an **additional 3-5 hours** to create the new concepts you're looking for, and it will most likely be **another 5-7 days** for me to get these back to you. Do you think it's worth it?

Client: I am not sure.

You: Personally, I like the design that you have now and it seems like you do as well. I'd suggest going with what we have in order to stay on time and on budget. What do you think?

I am not sure what I want, but if you create it I'll let you know.

Client is REALLY saying this to you, "I haven't done any homework on what's out there or what I might like. I'd like you to do all of the work for me."

You: I can appreciate that. Can you give me an idea of what you want?

Client: I'm not sure. I guess I'd have to think about it. I was kind of hoping you'd do this for me...

You: If you can, that's going to save us both a lot of time and money. It will also help you get this project done faster. I can develop concepts for you — it's part of the value I bring to the table. If you can provide me with some ideas, examples or inspiration that would point me in the right direction that would really help.

Client: I agree, but I am not really sure where to look.

You: That's no problem. If you have examples, or if you've seen something on the internet you like or don't like, that's a good place to start. Perhaps you can tell me about your competition's designs; could you tell me what you like and don't like about them?

Do you think it would be helpful if we look together at some examples, or would you like to look on your own? After you've had some time to think about what you've seen, we can get together and discuss it.

NOTE: Hearing, "*I am not sure what I want, but if you create it I'll know it*" should be an immediate red flag - sirens should be going off in your head telling you that you need to confidently yet gently instruct your client that you need their input to make this project a success.

Clients need to know that they're apart of the creative process as well; whether it's a logo a web site or something else — your ability to hit what they are looking for is a function of how much information they provide you up front.

Over the years I've lost hundreds of billable hours because I didn't gather the client's feedback/opinions/thoughts at the beginning of the project, instead I found myself "running around in the dark without a flashlight" trying to somehow create what the client was looking for. Unfortunately, I am not a mind reader (I am guessing you're not either), so make sure you educate your clients up-front that their project is a partnership that they need to be involved in as well. I think of something Gandalf the wizard said in the *Lord of the Rings* when asked to make a fire on a desolate mountain top, "*I can not burn snow, I must have something to work with.*" Creatively you should feel the same way, you too should have something to work with (a direction of some sort) before you start investing your time.

I think I might want you to go in a different direction.

Client is REALLY saying this to you, "I am frustrated with what you've come up with. My expectations haven't been met. I need you to steer this project back on course because I am losing confidence."

You: Before we put aside all of the work we've done so far, can you tell me what it is about the current design that you'd like to see changed? Do you know?

Client: I am not sure; it just seems to be missing something.

You: I appreciate your honesty. Let me ask you, what direction are you suggesting we go? Do you have an example of something you'd like the design to look like?

Client: At the moment, not really.

You: Before we go ahead and make some big changes in the design, I'd like to make sure we're not moving away from something that your ideal customers would like, since their opinion is what we really want to focus on. Do you think it would be wise for us to run the current design by a few of your best customers and see what they say before we change things up?

NOTE: This can be extremely frustrating to hear from a client, especially when you've invested a lot of time into her/his project. Control your emotions and focus on learning exactly what they want changed and why they want it changed. In taking this approach you both may find that you won't need to completely scrap your work, just make small changes.

Whether you live in a city the size of New York or London, it still is a small world.

If you burn people, it will inevitably come back to haunt you.

It looks like it needs something else. Can we add *blinking text and flashing lights?*

Client is REALLY saying this to you, "I don't like something about the design, but I have no idea what it is. Perhaps I might be a "closet designer" that could design if I chose to, but instead I'll use you as my instrument because I am creative."

NOTE: This would be an example of your client suddenly getting creative and providing you with ideas on how to make the project, *"better"*. Depending on your client's personality and your style, you may find that some clients feel they can and should provide you advice on how to do your job. Handling these *"well-meaning"* clients can be a bit tricky if you don't know how.

Remember that most of these clients only want to help, even though they might not be. You need to make sure you handle them confidently, professionally but gently.

You: Hmm, we can certainly look at something like that. Just so I know, what do you think that will do for the artwork?
What are your thoughts behind this idea?

Client: I am not sure. I just thought it would look good.

You: Well, it's not a bad idea, but the reason why I designed it as I did is because I've researched a number of your competitors. I am familiar with this industry, and I know that this design will attract the customers you are looking for. (*Be sure to list the reasons why the design is appropriate*).

OPTIONAL — More forceful:

You: I see what you're saying. All the same, I really think you'll get better results and the design will look better if we keep it as it is (*list your reasons again*). Do you think your ideal clients would agree?

OPTIONAL — Very forceful:

You: Well, we might be at an impasse here. My goal as a professional is to help you get the best design and result possible. That's why you hired me; for my experience and expertise, right?

Client: Yes.

You: I am advising you in my professional opinion that we leave the design as it is (*list your reasons again*). I think changing the design from what we have will result in you not getting as much value out of the project, and I'd hate to see that. In any case, before we make any changes, I'd suggest running this by your ideal clients and see what they might think. Wouldn't you agree?

NOTE: Sometimes, clients can provide wonderful insight, so listening to them will not only make them feel valued, but might also help you out. The danger lies in the client starting to think they are the

designer or creative director and you are their instrument. They just get over zealous and start coming up with "*new ideas that they want to try.*" This typically means huge headaches for you.

Remember, you're the expert. You don't want to be rude to the client, but the whole reason he or she hired you was to bring creativity to the table, not mock up the ideas they have spinning in their head. When you're first interviewing a client, you should be able spot tendencies like this. If you do, be careful.

We have to wait for Judy, our marketing manager to approve it before we can give you the go ahead. Everyone here was okay with it, but she might like to see some changes.

Client is REALLY saying this to you, "I can't or won't make this decision on my own. Perhaps I'd like to have a safety net in case we decide to change something."

You: Sure. Since we're almost completely through the project at this point, you aren't expecting Judy to suggest that we make major changes to the project, are you?

Client: I don't think so, but I can't be certain.

You: Mind reading is tough, I know! Let's see what kinds of changes (if any) are requested, and we'll talk about them before moving forward. We'll want to make sure we're not making drastic changes to the project when we're really in the process of wrapping it up. That might easily cause us to go over budget and time.

So I can plan my schedule and make sure your project gets done when we agreed it would, can you let me know when Judy will give us the go ahead?

I was talking to *my neighbor,* and *he* said we should change this. Can we?

Client is REALLY saying this to you, "I don't completely trust your design or my judgment for this project, so I wanted to get other opinions from others, and they suggested you go in a different direction."

You: Getting feedback from others is always a good idea. Just be sure to get feedback from your customers, rather than friends and family. Since customers are the ones that buy from you, it's critical to know what they think. Does that make sense?

Client: Yeah, I just like to get other people's opinions too.

You: Getting feedback from friends and family is a bit of a double-edged sword: I've seen it help clients, but more often than not, it adds a lot of confusion. In order to make sure you get the best return on your investment with this project, we'll want to focus on just what your ideal customers say.

Client: I understand, but my neighbor's son who is a designer made the comment that while he liked the colors, he wasn't crazy about the font.

You: I designed your flyer based on the conversations we've had about what you like and what your ideal customers will respond to. I feel confident you'll find they like what we've created, don't you?

Have you shown this design to your customers yet? If you have, what do they say, and how do they feel about it?

NOTE: Again, this is a delicate situation; you don't want to come off as rude and obnoxious, but at the same time you don't want to be taking orders from a sideline, amateur freelancer who's sticking their nose where it doesn't belong. Be polite and avoid getting rattled by their feedback, instead reestablish your expertise as successful, time-tested freelancer who does these types of projects everyday. Indicate that getting feedback from people outside the industry can often make things more confusing and frustrating. If they must get opinions from other people about their project have them talk to their customers rather than a friend, sibling or pet that has no idea what they are talking about.

I changed my mind; I'd like to go back to the way that it was.

Client is REALLY saying this to you, "I am indecisive and I may not see (or care) that changing my mind causes you to lose time and money."

You: No problem. I know sometimes people change their mind on things. What caused you to rethink this? Is there any chance you'll change your mind again?

Client: I don't know; I guess I thought it would look better but it doesn't.

You: I agree with you — good call. Just keep in mind that we can burn up a lot of time going back and forth here, so let me know if you're sure this is what you want to do. This way we save time and continue to move towards hitting your project deadline.

NOTE: Depending on the circumstances, this may be a big deal or it may not. Hopefully you'll have the ability to go back to what they had before. If not, you'll need to take this in another direction. Do make a point of making backups on a regular basis though — it will save you a tremendous amount of hassle.

The important point here is that you educate your client that changing their mind frequently will slow the project down.

Clients often don't see that changing their mind requires work and effort on your part. This is a nice way to remind them.

When good people have a falling out, only one of them may be at fault at first; but if the strife continues long, usually both become guilty.

—Thomas Fuller, 1608-1661, British Clergyman, Author

I'd like to make just a few more changes, and then we might be good.

Client is REALLY saying this to you, "I want you to make more changes, but I am leaving the door open, just in case I want to add more later."

You: Sounds great. What I'd suggest you do is make a list of all of the final changes that you'll have for the project. You can send over an email with the list or we can talk about them on the phone. When might you be able to get those over to me?

Client: Probably on Friday.

You: Terrific, I'll plan it. Once I know what the remaining fixes are, I'll get to work. When I'm done, I will contact you, we'll verify they've been done and we'll get the project wrapped up for you. How does that sound?

NOTE: This is an important move to learn because clients often keep requesting changes over and over again. It's a lot like a little kid that keeps popping coins into a ride at the carnival. Sure, you want to be patient; just be careful that you don't get on this "carousel of changes" that you can't get off of.

The best way to handle this is to let them know they should list all of their changes, get them over to you and then you'll wrap it up. It's critical that you put a limit on the number of changes clients will be allowed. How many that number is, up to you: some clients you might be more lenient with than others.

I don't have time to proof the advertisement. I am sure it's fine; go ahead and send it to the printer.

Client is REALLY saying this to you, "I am too busy or too lazy to look at the proof. Perhaps the proof seems like a formality. If there is a mistake, I will still hold you accountable."

You: Yeah, I know the day can get hectic with other things. All the same, it probably won't take you more than a couple of minutes to look this over one last time and make sure we've got it right.

Client: Yeah, I know, but I've just got so much going on today.

You: This is your call, but we've worked hard on this project and I know it's going to be expensive to rerun the ad if it's printed with a problem you didn't notice. Do you think it's worth it to spend a few minutes looking it over and maybe running it by one or two other people before you approve it?

OPTIONAL — I highly recommend you have the client sign an approval form or at least send you an email that the final design has been officially approved:

You: Before I go ahead and send the artwork to print, I'll ask you to fax or email over a document that states that this project is "*approved and is ready to go to print.*" Okay?

Client: Sure, but why do I need to do this?

You: I do this with all projects that are going to print. This serves as a record that you had the opportunity to look over and approve the artwork one last time before it went to print. It'll take you just a couple of minutes to get it over to me. Once I have it I'll get the artwork sent out later today.

NOTE: All of this seems pretty Innocuous, doesn't it? Be careful here, many a freelancer has been burned badly by an example just like this.

Whether you're making a web site live, submitting an advertisement to the yellow pages or sending in a final brochure to a printer, avoid doing them at all costs until you've received the "official" go ahead by your client.

Additionally, you should ask that your client submit this request over fax or email so you have written documentation.

This sounds silly...I know, but submitting projects without written final approval from your client is like playing with fire: sooner or later you're going to get burned.

I know we approved the current design, but we asked a few of our friends and they have suggested some changes.

Client is REALLY saying this to you, "We changed our minds and if we downplay it, perhaps we won't be charged extra."

You: It's always wise to get feedback, so I am glad you had the opportunity to do so. If the changes are minor and won't take more than a few minutes to make I'll be happy to do them for you as a freebie so we can get to a final version. If the changes are significant and require more than 30 minutes to complete, we will need to add a little more to the balance to compensate for the extra work. Does that sound fair?

Client: I thought that would have been included in the package. Are you really going to charge me?

You: I am guessing the changes your friends recommended won't be that drastic, so we'll probably be okay. What we'll want to do is examine the changes and see which ones might require a significant amount of rework. Based on what you're looking to change, we can decide which changes are worth investing in and which ones aren't.

Client: That's fine, but I thought we could keep making revisions if we needed to.

You: I am always happy to accommodate quick changes once or twice during the initial phase of the project. However, once the web

If you are planning on doing business with someone again, don't be too tough in the negotiations.

If you're going to skin a cat, don't keep it as a house cat.

— Marvin S. Levin

site is approved, we move on from the conceptualization phase to production and building. When changes are requested in this phase they often require a lot of rework, which is not included in the initial budget and time line.

Again, I'll be happy to talk with you about the changes you have and see what can be done for you. I want to make sure that all of my clients are happy, but allowing unlimited revisions would cause the price to skyrocket, and I want to make this affordable as well.

NOTE: You'll have to be careful with this one. The client may be trying to take advantage of you, or they may just be asking this out of ignorance. Try not to assume the worst.

Client Demands and Verbal Choke Holds:
Extending the Project Scope

Can you contact *my web host* and help me sort this out?

Client is REALLY saying this to you, "I can't do this or just don't want to. Can you take care of it, preferably for free?"

You: Well, what exactly would you like me to do?

Client: I've worked with these guys before and I need you to call them and coordinate this project for me.

OPTION A — Nice version:

You: Just to let you know, I typically charge a reasonable fee for providing technical support like this. I like working with you, and if we can handle this quickly I will waive the charge this time.
How does that sound?

Send the client an invoice after you do the work, even if the bill is for $0. This lets the client know that you invested your time and you value it as well.

OPTION B — More forceful version:

You: Just to let you know, I typically charge a reasonable fee for providing technical support like this. It's usually not very much but I do have to account for my time. How can I help you?

Client: I guess I'll need you to figure out why my web mail isn't working. I need you to call my web host, log into my account and figure out what is going wrong.

You: No problem. I am guessing that will take me just an hour or two. Now you can always give them a call yourself and they'll probably be able to help you out. I know their technical support is good, and it won't cost you a dime. If you'd like me to step in and provide support, it will be just $125. Is that something you'll want me to do?

NOTE: Maybe calling your client's web host or printer is within your current project scope. If it is, this section will not apply to you.

However, if you are not currently working on a project for a client, and he or she unexpectedly contacts you and wants you to step in and solve a problem for them, you'll need to let them know that your time and expertise will cost them money.

Of course, you should step in and help them if you've directly or indirectly caused the problem.

You'll find that a certain percentage of clients will try to get you to do work for free for them. They won't come right out and say, "*I expect this for free*", but it's implied.

The client may feel that you owe them because they've done business with you before, or they assume "it's easy" so no one should be charged for it.

The fact is, if it "*was easy*" they would be able to do it themselves.

Be careful trying to fix somebody else's problem. It's difficult to know the exact problem as it exists in someone else's mind.

Quarrels would not last so long if the fault lay only on one side.

— Francois De La Rochefoucauld, 1613-1680, French Classical Writer

Will I be able to contact you after hours or on weekends if I need to?

Client is REALLY saying this to you, "I need to make sure I have access to you when I need you, no matter when that may be."

You: Like most businesses I do have regular office hours. It's important that I have some time to recharge my creative battery so I can continue to provide outstanding design. You'll have almost no trouble reaching me Monday through Friday from 8-5.

With good project planning, I've found that almost all of my clients get what they want, when they want it, so working nights and weekends isn't necessary. Are you expecting that you'll need to reach me at night and on weekends?

Client: I might need to. Will I be able to?

You: On extremely rare occasions, I have offered clients weekend accessibility at a premium of one and a half times my normal rate, so we'd be looking at $135 per hour. This is subject to me being available, but if you're in this position, let me know and I'll see if I can help.

I don't have the materials you need, so you will have to get the files from my previous freelancer.

Client is REALLY saying this to you, "I don't know what you are looking for and or I am not interested in learning. Instead, I want you to handle all the details yourself."

You: Since I don't know the arrangement you had with this freelancer, I might not be the best person to step in and contact them. I would be happy to help, but from past experience I will tell you that sometimes this can be a little tricky if your previous freelancer doesn't want to cooperate. I can give you a list of the information you'll need to get and you can contact him or her. Does that make sense?

Client: It makes sense but I would rather you handle it. I don't really understand all of this stuff.

You: If it's imperative that I coordinate with your previous freelancer, I would just ask that you contact them first and let them know that I will be contacting them. I've found that most freelancers appreciate this courtesy.

If you provide them with a rough idea of what we'll be looking for it will give them a little time to prepare the information we'll need, so we'll be able to speed the process up for everyone. Is this something you'll be able to do?

NOTE: The thing to be careful of here is getting in between an angry freelancer and client. Perhaps the reason why this client is working with you instead of the previous freelancer is because of a misunderstanding, argument or perhaps the reason is actually legitimate and the client just doesn't technically know what to ask for. Whatever the case, you just want to protect yourself from refereeing a boxing match between previous freelancer and client.

MH

Can you come in for a meeting at my office?

Client is REALLY saying this to you, "I'd rather you drive than me. I am more concerned with my time than yours."

You: What would you like to accomplish in the meeting?

Client: I'd just like to bounce some ideas I have for the project off you, and see what ideas you might have.

You: It sounds like we'll be able to accomplish the same thing and save some time and money by having a teleconference instead. This way I won't need to bill for travel expenses and we can both save some time.

Client: Okay.

You: Since we're doing this by phone, my schedule will be a lot more open. I am available to teleconference at Thursday at 9:00 AM or Friday at 1:00 PM. Which one will work the best for you?

NOTE: The client doesn't put any value on your travel time, so let them know that you are trying to save them from having to pay for it; this assigns value. Then you can move to a solution that is just as good, but won't cost them anything for a quick decision.

Can you take a look at the text on my web site and make any corrections that you see?

Client is REALLY saying this to you, "I'd like you to proofread my project, even if it's not within the project scope, preferably for free."

You: Sure, I'd be happy to help you out. This is called copy editing and it's an additional service I provide clients that need a little more than an extra set of eyes to look at their project.

Client: Well, I think it's pretty clean. I just want you to look at it and tell me what you think is wrong.

You: I understand. It will probably take me about 45 minutes to go through what you have. I can then provide you with a list of suggestions. I can get this done for you in two days, and it won't run you more than $50. Do you think it's worth the investment to have this done or would you rather take a peek at it yourself?

OR:

You: I'd love to help, but this is a little outside my area of expertise. I would suggest that we look at bringing in the services of a professional copy editor.

Client: Okay, but that sounds expensive. What would you suggest?

You: Don't worry. I know of an excellent content editing company called Creating Words that Sell. I am sure they will be able to help and their rates are pretty reasonable. Would you like me to forward you their contact information or set up a teleconference for the three of us?

I have some pictures to use in the project. Can you scan them in or do some retouching?

Client is REALLY saying this to you, "Do you have the capability to do this for me? I'd rather not have to do this myself or hire someone else to do this. I am not sure if I should pay for this or not."

OPTION A — You want to help out:

You: Sure, I can do that for you. It's a bit outside our project scope but I can help out. I am guessing, based on what you've told me about the pictures, that it will take me about 45 minutes.

Client: Can you give me an idea how much it will cost me?

You: I can probably keep the cost below $75. Would you like to consider some other options, or would you like me to go ahead and get it done for you?

OPTION B — You don't want to help out, or you can't help out:

You: Well, I might not be the right fit for this, but if you want, I can do some checking around and find someone you can contact that will be able to help you. If I can get some contact information over to you by end of business tomorrow, would that work for you?

NOTE: As you've probably noticed throughout this section, clients often don't place value on your services. It's your job to educate them (in a nice way) that there is value to this service and that you have to charge for it unless it was included in the project scope. You should have a list of resources available if you want to help the client out but don't want to do the work yourself.

It's pretty easy to upload video to the internet, right? Can you do that for me?

Client is REALLY saying this to you, "Even though I can't or won't do this, I don't see that it's all that difficult. I'll probably put pressure on you to give me this for free or at a discount."

You: It shouldn't be too bad. Let me see, I'll need to get the footage off of the video camera onto the computer, encode the video as well as compress it for the internet, and finally upload it to my server... It

We must not contradict, but instruct him that contradicts us; for a madman is not cured by another running mad also.

— Antisthenes, 388-311 BC, Greek Dramatist

should take me between 3-5 hours depending on how much footage I'll be working with.

NOTE: It's important not to argue with the client about how easy or difficult this really is. Instead, spell out exactly what it will take to accomplish the task.

Clients often intentionally or unintentionally omit — or just don't know about — steps which cause them to think the task is much easier than it really is.

Can you help me figure out *why my computer is crashing?*

Client is REALLY saying this to you, "I may be confused, hoping for a quick answer, desperate for someone to help or I may just be trying to get something for free."

NOTE: When asked to perform services you aren't skilled at, it's important that you have resources you can readily provide them rather than feel obligated to perform the work for them.

You: Well, this doesn't sound like a design issue per se, and it's not really my area of expertise but I do know of someone that would be able to help you out in this area. I know they provide great work and I've heard their fees are quite reasonable. Would you like me to forward over their contact information?

OR — If you do want to help them:

You: I can take a look at this; it will probably only take 2-3 hours. I can start it in within the next three days. Would you like me to go ahead and get that started or would you like to hold off for now?

NOTE: The client may be implying that you do this for free because he or she doesn't value the work. It's your responsibility to assign value to it and have them decide if it's worth it.

Can we swap out some of the stock photos you used in my project? I want to swap out the pictures of the dog and the woman.

NOTE: There are times that the client has a legitimate reason for wanting or needing another stock photo used. Try to be accommodating if you can. If what they're asking for can't be done, or if it'll cost you a lot of time and money you'll want to go with the approach below.

You: We can always go in that direction, but before I jump into it, I chose the dog because the shot is downright funny, and of all of the photos I had access to, it was the best.
With the other shot, the woman looks friendly and fits your target demographic perfectly. Let me ask you, is there something specific you're not seeing with these photos or are you just interested in trying out some other images?

Client: I like the dog but I thought having him on one leg would really be funny. The shot of the woman is okay; I just wondered if there was a better photo out there.

You: Okay... We have a couple of different options here depending on your budget. Since these photos came from my stock library they're no charge. We can certainly invest some time looking at stock photo galleries online to find what you're looking for.
It'll probably take us 30-45 minutes, and the photos will run us about $10 each. I am not sure swapping the photos out will affect sales all that much but I am happy to go this direction if you want. Do you feel it's worth the extra time and money?

Client: No, let's just stick with what we have in there now.

NOTE: Notice how significantly tying the client's decisions to money affects the outcome can be.

When applicable, you always want to tie additional work, energy, photos, etc. to money. More time on your part = more money on their part.

Hey, you deal with computers, can you tell me why *my laptop can't connect to the internet?*

Client is REALLY saying this to you, "I am too lazy or too cheap to hire someone. I figured I'd hit you up for a freebie and see if I get lucky."

You: I do work with computers, but my area of specialty really is graphic design, and what you're looking for is technical support. When I run into a challenge like this with my computer I usually jump on the internet and search for what other people are saying about it.

There's an unbelievable amount of free information from experts that really know what they're doing on there; you just need to be a little patient. Try typing in *"laptop WIFI problems"*, or visit your laptop manufacturer's web site. They almost always have great support for this type of issue since you can't be the only one that's run into this.

Client: I'll check into that, but can you give me some advice on what you think it is?

You: I could speculate, but I am just not an expert in this area.
If I am not 100% confident in my advice I'd rather not give it — the last thing I want to do is send you on a wild goose chase, or make your situation worse.

I really would check online and see what you come up with. If that still doesn't work you can always call a professional IT tech who deals with these types of issues on a daily basis.

MH

In your "infinite wisdom" as a talented freelancer, I'm guessing this will probably only take you *about 5 minutes, right?*

Client is REALLY saying this to you, "I'll try to make you feel guilty or foolish charging me for what I believe is something I shouldn't be billed for. I'll do this by first complimenting you and then implying that it's a quick and easy task."

You: Hey thanks for the kind words. I am not quite sure if I'll be able to get this small project done in only 5 minutes. That would be impressive, but I should be able to keep it to around 15 or 20 (*consider listing the steps you will actually need to perform*). For these smaller projects I typically charge a nominal fee of just $25 for my "*infinite wisdom*" and small time investment.

Client: Are you really going to charge me for this even though it'll only take a few minutes?

You: Nah, this one I'll let go as a freebie (*you may offer this, or you may just decide to charge her/him, it's up to you*), but I do want to point out that just like other professionals, I bill not only for my time but also for my expertise. For example, a doctor may see you for 10 minutes but bill you several hundred dollars. Does that make sense?

NOTE: Notice how the client compliments you right before asking you for a favor. This may be a coincidence, but remember the old phrase — "*you always catch more bees with honey than vinegar.*"

To handle this effectively, thank your client quickly for the compliment and move on to business. Avoid being rude or ungrateful towards the compliment, but if you feel the client is just "*buttering*" you up so you'll do some work for free, make sure you keep your response focused. Notice the response to the client also uses humor as a bit of a weapon.

Keep in mind that it's not only the actual time you invest in a project that you need to charge for but the EXPERTISE it took you to become that proficient. Maybe something that now takes you 5 minutes would take a rookie in the field 2 hours. Avoid falling into the trap that just because something was quick means you shouldn't bill for it.

Client Demands and Verbal Choke Holds:
Billing

> *We pay people on the first of each month. You need to talk to the accounts payable department to get paid.*
>
> Client is REALLY saying this to you, "I am unwilling to help you. If I pulled some strings, I might be able to get the money, but I don't want to deal with it."

You: I know that some companies have strict accounts payable procedures, and I want to respect yours. If you bill only on the first, fifteenth, or last of the month I understand. I'll hold off on getting the double-sided flyer started until the next pay cycle.

Client: When will you be able to get started?
What if I need it sooner?

You: Once I've received the check, I'll put you back into the schedule and get your project started within 3 days. If you need the project sooner, I'd suggest talking to someone in your accounts payable department to see if they can make an exception. I've had a number of clients that were able to do this in special circumstances.

NOTE: In some cases larger clients will stick to their guns on this issue and you'll need to make a decision on whether it's worth it to let them pay you the way they want to. For smaller companies you'll have a little more flexibility and leverage (but don't expect them to make it easy on you if they are used to paying at a certain time).

As in almost all of these responses, it's crucial that you be able to accurately analyze your situation, your "*opponent*" and your leverage. Based on all of these factors you make an educated decision on which way to go.

I need these business cards to go to the printer today, and I'll pay you in next month's billing cycle.

Client is REALLY saying this to you, "I need you to make good on this deal now and trust that I'll hold up my end of the bargain later. By telling you about my company's billing cycle, I hope to convince you that there's nothing I can do."

You: If money is a problem right now, we'll take care of the design balance and hold off sending the artwork to the printer until the funds are available. You might not be aware of this, but when the artwork is sent to the printer, I am sent a bill that has to be paid immediately.

MH

Client: I didn't know that.

You: If the printer runs the job and has difficulty collecting funds, they are out time, money and material. That's why they collect before the job goes to print, and that's why I do the same. Does that make sense to you? Why not put the balance on a credit card if your money situation is tight right now?

Client: I suppose that might work.

You: Would you like to handle the balance today or would you like to hold off until funds become available?

I never pay a cent until we see the final product...or, Send over the final files and we'll issue a check.

Client is REALLY saying this to you, "I am worried or just flat out refuse to be stuck with something I don't want. I might have been burned in the past by a designer, or I don't understand how the design / billing process works."

You: I know getting these files quickly is important to you. As per our agreement, as soon as we receive funds I will make the files available to you in 24-48 hours.

We can go ahead and take payment right now if you're ready. I just need a credit or debit card. If that won't work, I can send over a PayPal invoice or you can have a courier deliver a check.

You punch me, I punch back. I do not believe it's good for ones self-respect to be a punching bag.
— **Edward Koch, 1924-, American Politician**

Which option is going to be best for you?

Client: I've never had that arrangement in the past.

You: I can appreciate that. All the same, I follow what industry professionals have adopted as policy for years — I collect the balance due before the files are provided. In the past, I've never had a client that objected to this part of our agreement.
Is there a reason why this might be a problem for you?

NOTE: Avoid getting into the argument that once you release the files, they don't have to pay you. This is true, but it's not worth bringing up. Just focus on the idea that this is your process and this is how it's done. If the client truly does need the files in a hurry they will have NO problem getting you the funds.

The check is in the mail; I don't know why you haven't received it.

Client is REALLY saying this to you, "I need to buy myself some time. If the check doesn't arrive, I can just say that the post office lost it or claim that I didn't know what happened."

You: I am not sure. You never know what can happen with the post office.

Client: Yeah, I don't know, I put it in the mail.

You: Why don't we do this? If I haven't received the check by tomorrow, I will give you a call, and you can pay the balance over the phone with a credit card. Otherwise, I can come over **between 12:00 and 1:00 tomorrow** and pick up the check, or I can send a courier over **between 2:00 and 4:00 tomorrow** to pick up the check. Which option will work best for you?

OR:

You: I am not sure. I've checked the mail every day but I haven't received it. You never quite know what to expect from the local post office.

Client: Hmm, I am not sure either. I guess you can't trust the post office.

You: I do need to handle this balance today, so what I suggest we do is to put a stop payment on the check. I can take a credit card payment over the phone or I can send a courier to your office at 2:30 today and pick it up from you. Which option would be a better fit for you?

Client: If I have to choose, a credit card I guess.

NOTE: If you and the client agree to handle the matter the next day, make sure you've agreed on an exact time this will happen. After you agree on the time, repeat it to the client: *"Okay, so you'll be available at 12:00 tomorrow so I can come by and pick up the check, right?"*

I've had clients tell me this all the time. Sadly, most of them weren't telling the truth — the check never did arrive; they were just stalling for time. The important thing here is not to accuse them of lying. Avoid arguing with them. Instead let them off the hook this one time and then suggest a few fair options that will absolutely ensure you'll get paid the next day.

When my venture capital comes in, I'll be able to get some money to you.

Client is REALLY saying this to you, "I am going to make paying you conditional on some external factor. Even though it was not listed in the agreement, I am hoping you'll go along."

You: Thanks for the heads up. I appreciate you keeping me in the loop, but ultimately it's really none of my business what's going on outside of this project and what we've agreed upon.

Client: I was just letting you know. Money is kind of tight right now.

You: I understand. I have your next payment due on Monday, the 21st. Are you still planning to pay me at this time?

Client: It might be tough.

You: I appreciate your honesty. However, we've both agreed that you would pay me at this time, so I do need to be paid on this date. If you want, you can put the balance on a credit card or secure a short term loan. Whatever direction you decide to go is up to you. I do rely on these payments so I can pay my bills, so I would appreciate you honoring our agreement and making sure I do get paid when promised.

NOTE: Sometimes clients really do just want to keep you in the loop and let you know that they will pay you on time. On the other hand, I've worked with clients that used this excuse as a shield so they aren't held accountable for the agreement they made.

They feel if they can tie your payment to an outside event that's beyond their control, you just have to wait for the event to happen, since *"there's nothing they can do about it."* This is rubbish; don't get suckered into this. Instead, politely let them know that their activities beyond your contract are really none of your business or concern, and that you expect them to honor the agreement you both made.

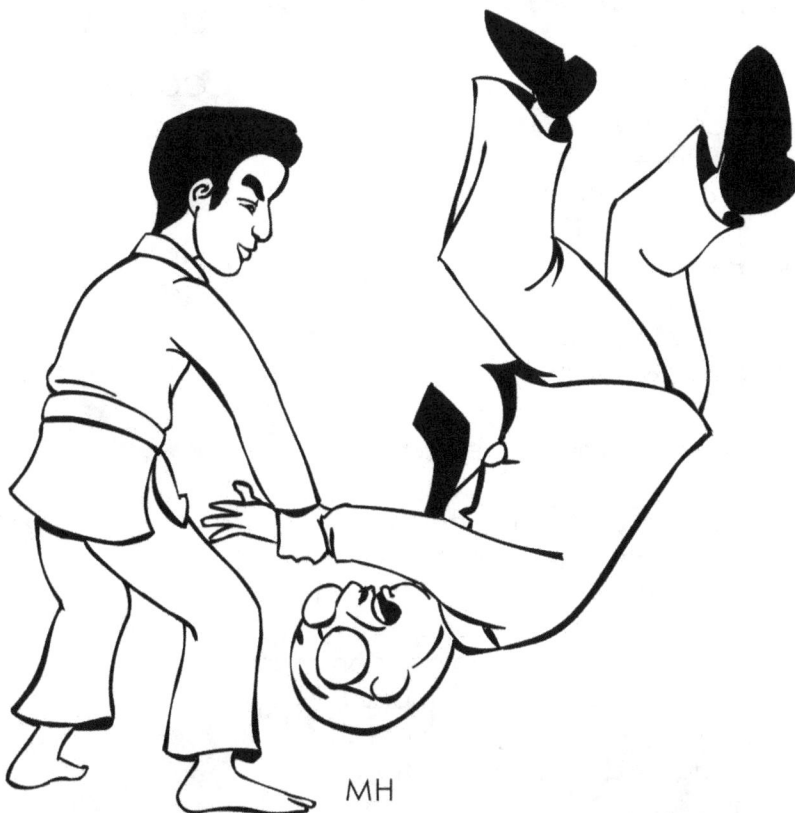

MH

I need to handle these bills first and then I can pay you.

Client is REALLY saying this to you, "I am attempting to change the payment terms of our agreement. I'm hoping you will let it slide."

OPTION A — Nice version:

You: I appreciate your willingness to pay the invoice. It looks like your next payment of $750 is due on Monday, March 15. I know other bills can sometimes be an issue, but having you pay me on time would be very much appreciated.

ALSO — If you wish to compromise further:

You: It sounds like you'll just need a bit more time to take care of this, right? Why don't I do this: I'll fax over a little addendum to our agreement that states you'll be able to provide the amount due by Monday, March 22. We'll both sign it and we'll move on. Does that sound like something that will work for you?

OPTION B — Forceful version:

You: I appreciate your willingness to pay the invoice. Per our agreement, the payment of $750 will be due on Monday, March 15. If you have other accounts payable commitments, you might consider placing the balance on a credit card. In any case, I'll need you to pay me the amount we agreed to, on the date we agreed on.

Better a friendly refusal than an unwilling consent.

— **Spanish Proverb**

If I put the check in the mail today, will you be able to send out the artwork?

Client is REALLY saying this to you, "I want the artwork right now, and while I know you need to get paid before you deliver the artwork, I am asking that you trust me."

You: I know you're excited to get the project finished up, and I want to get the artwork out as soon as possible. We did agree (in the contract) that payment was to be made before the final artwork was delivered, but I have a couple of options I think will provide an easy solution.

Client: I do need the artwork, so what do you have in mind?

You: If you need the artwork delivered today, you could (list only the options below that are acceptable to you):

- Drop the check off
- Meet me somewhere to make payment
- Hire a courier to deliver the check
- Make a PayPal payment
- Pay with a credit or debit card

Which of these options will work best for you?

NOTE: Make sure in your contract that you have a clause that says that the final artwork will be delivered or uploaded when the final payment has been received.

You might want to let a client slide on this, but personally, I would never release the final artwork until you've been paid. If they want the artwork badly enough, they WILL find a way to get the payment to you.

CP

I can't pay you up front. I need to be able to make payments on the balance or I have to go elsewhere.

Client is REALLY saying this to you, "I don't have or don't want to pay the money up front. Perhaps I don't want (or can't get) credit somewhere else."

You: If you need to finance this project, I'd recommend going with an institution that specializes in extending credit to small businesses, such as a bank or credit union. You could even use a credit card.

Client: Why can't you offer payments?

You: I suppose that's something that could be looked into. However, credit card companies and banks are much more equipped to handle financing than you or I as small business owners. Wouldn't you agree?

Client: Perhaps, but I really do need the payments.

You: I can sympathize with you. Being able to pay in installments makes things easier and does minimize your risk a little bit.

I've found that business owners who truly believe in their company and vision, and have decent credit power, have no problems finding someone who will be more than happy to extend them credit. It sounds like you would be in that category; can you see any reason why you may have trouble placing the balance on a credit card?

NOTE: There of course may be other reasons why the client wants you to extend them financing terms. If you feel it will help your business you may consider it. Just be aware that if they default (and sooner or later someone will), you will have to collect the money yourself, hire a collections firm or hire an attorney.

The bottom line is, if you can get them to pay up front, do it. You may even consider offering a discount for balances paid up front.

Client Demands and Verbal Choke Holds:
Project Printing Problems

The colors on my brochure came out dull or different compared to my computer screen. What can be done about this?

Client is REALLY saying this to you, "I don't like what I see here, or this project didn't meet my expectations. what are you going to do about it?"

NOTE: This is another example of something you should have in your contract, just in case something like this arises. You'll also want to educate your client early in the process that his or her monitor was almost surely not calibrated correctly, so what they see isn't necessarily going to be what they get.

Many clients don't want to pay for exact color matching, printed proofs and spot colors, and yet they'll complain about color shifting. What you might want to do is first look at the artwork; see if the client's got a point. Clients looking to save money on printing must accept some degree of color shifting. By seeing the artwork firsthand, you'll be able to make an assessment if the color shift is or isn't outside the realm of what the colors should be.

Until you see the artwork, it's best to give the client the benefit of the doubt.

You: I am sorry to hear that. Would you mind if I took a couple of minutes here to clear up some confusion about color on a monitor versus a printed piece?

Client: Fine, I just need some answers.

You: You see, computer monitors reproduce color differently than what we see on a printed piece of paper. Color monitors can reproduce a much wider range of colors and brightness; much more than we can achieve on a printed piece. That's why you might look at a printed piece and think it looks dull compared to the way it looks on the computer monitor.

Client: Okay...

You: To complicate things further, it's critical that you have a high-end monitor to view your artwork on, and that it's properly calibrated. You can purchase professional hardware and software to help you do this; often clients might report that the colors look slightly different on their printed piece compared to their monitor. When that happens, there's a good chance their monitor was not calibrated. Am I correct in assuming you haven't had your monitor professionally calibrated?

Client: No, it hasn't been calibrated.

You: I know you wanted to stay within a specific budget for this project, so in order to do that we needed to go this direction and have your project printed the way we did. The advantage is that we saved you a ton of money. The trade off is that we don't have perfect control over the colors, and they can shift a little bit. Most clients, when they hear how much it will cost to get exact colors, immediately decide to go with the less precise method and take the huge cost savings.

Client: How much would it have cost me to run this project right, so I would have gotten the colors I wanted?

You: In your case, we ended up **saving about $500 - $750** on printing costs. If we would have insisted the colors be exactly what we set them out to be, also called color matching, it would have pushed our budget to **three times more** than what it was. I know the colors weren't exactly what you thought they would be. Would it have been worth it to pay **three times** what you did, or do you think it was wise that we went with the more inexpensive option?

Always provide your clients with both options as the project begins: high-end color matching or budget gang / bulk runs that save money. Explain the pros and cons of each and let them decide which direction to go.
Sensei say, *"If retribution you fear, always cover your rear."*

My project didn't get done when I needed it, so I don't think I should pay for it.

Client is REALLY saying this to you, "You or your printer didn't meet my expectations, so I should get something in return. I might not get the full refund, but I am going to suggest it — the worst the designer can say is 'No.'"

NOTE: This one can be a tricky one, so be careful how you handle it. If you agreed, either verbally or in the proposal, to complete the project for a specific event at a specific time, and were not able to deliver, you might be at fault.

Of course, you will want to check with your attorney. In this case we're looking at how to respond to a client who did not specify a deadline and is probably just upset that he or she didn't receive the artwork sooner.

You: Well, I do feel badly about that. I guess I'd have to ask you though, when did you need it and why wasn't this brought up when we were creating the agreement?

Client: I found out in the middle of the project that I needed it by November 24.

You: Again, I am sorry to hear this. When we created and signed our agreement on November 13th, there was no mention of this deadline. We agreed that the artwork was to be delivered by November 30.

While I feel badly it didn't work out quite the way you wanted it, the project parameters seem to have changed after we agreed on them.

People who treat other people as less than human must not be surprised when the bread they have cast on the waters comes floating back to them, poisoned.

— James Baldwin, 1924-1987, American Author

Client: Still, I just don't think this is fair.

You: I understand. If the artwork was only going to be used for a specific event at a specific time, we should have specifically outlined this in the agreement. Since we didn't, I am not sure how you can ask for a refund. Are you saying that you can't use the artwork at all now?

I need to make a change to the artwork. I know it's been sent to the printer, but is there anything we can do?

Client is REALLY saying this to you, "I found a change or error I want to address. I know I've signed off on the project, but I'm going to try to get this fixed anyway."

You: Let me place a call to the printer and see if it's been run yet. There is an outside chance that we'll be in luck, but it's likely the job has already been run, so we'll need to come up with another option.

Client: Anything you can do would be great.

You: Gotcha. Now I can't promise anything, but I'll see what I can do. Assuming the project hasn't already run, It should take me about 30 minutes to make the change, prepare the final file and send it back to the printer. This will run you just $35. Is it worth it to change, assuming the printer hasn't already run the job?

Client: Well, I've got to get this done so I don't have much of a choice. What if the project's already been printed?

You: If the job has been run, the printer will of course bill for the job since they are out paper, labor and ink. I can still make the change and we can rerun the job if you feel we need to. I can also check with the printer to see if he or she will be able to provide us with a discount or rush job to help the situation out a little. Does that sound fair?

NOTE: Here's where you might want to throw your client a bone and give them a little freebie since they just had to pay for printing they don't want. This is a judgment call you need to make; If you want to help out try this:

You: I can go ahead and make the changes for you. Normally this would run $50, but I'll do them **for half off this time.** I'll contact the printer to see if we can get the corrected project on the press as soon as possible so we can get this into your hands. Is it worth making the change or do you think it's best to stay with what we currently have?

I have a deadline, so I need you to call the printer and get them to run my job right now.

Client is REALLY saying this to you, "Things have changed on my end, and I am feeling stressed or pressured. I may not realize that I may be responsible for rush charges if I ask for this."

NOTE: A client may say this for a number of different reasons. If the client was late with the artwork, try the following:

You: I know deadlines are important, and making this deadline is important to both of us. The way printers typically work is that they put jobs in the queue as they arrive. Sometimes they will look at the complexity and scope of the job as well. It's challenging since everyone wants their project done first.

Client: Okay, but I just need this project back as quickly as possible.

You: I understand. I am excited to see how this project turns out as well. To ensure everyone's project gets done as quickly and efficiently as possible, printers will assign every project, yours included, a place in the queue based on when your job came in. Typically, it is first come, first printed.

Client: Is there anything you can do?

You: I'll be happy to contact the printer and see if anything can be done. They might be able to offer us a little help if it's a slow day. But in my experience, it's difficult to suddenly push a rush through when the day has already been planned out. If the printer is unable to accommodate us, we'll want to look into other options.

Why don't I give them a call and see what can be done? Will that work for you?

NOTE: If the printer is late getting their job done, try this:

You: I know there is a deadline on this project, so I'll call and see what the status of the job is and what can be done if they are running late. I know sometimes things don't work out exactly as planned with printers, and just like everyone else, they might get a little behind. If they are running late, I will express to them our urgency and see what they can do to get us back on track. Does that sound all right to you?

Client Demands and Verbal Choke Holds:
Copyrights and Master Files

What if I want to make changes to my project in the future?

Client is REALLY saying this to you, "Am I going to have access to these files? I don't want to have to pay someone to recreate the entire project every time I have changes. Can you help me understand this?"

You: Good question. Just let me know what changes will need to be made and I'll get them done for you quickly. The cost for the fixes is just $75 per hour for making changes to current files.

Most fixes can be done with less than one hour of labor time, and I can typically get them back to you within two business days.

OPTIONAL:

You: For the time, hassle and aggravation it will probably take you to do them, it might be easier just to have me handle the fixes. I've had clients inquire about this before, but when they realize what's involved in making it happen they decide it's best not to get involved with it.

Client: Out of curiosity, what would I need to do?

You: In order to make the changes, you would have to purchase professional design software, which can cost hundreds or thousands of dollars. You would also have to budget a considerable amount of time to learn the software.

It's kind of like doing your own automobile repairs: most people feel that it isn't worth it, and it's better to let a pro do it. Do you think it's worth the trouble?

I've already paid you for the work, so why don't I get it?

Client is REALLY saying this to you, "I don't understand all of this stuff about rights; I believe you owe me everything. You need to explain this to me or give me the files."

You: Let me take a moment and clear up some confusion. Just like a professional photographer or other contracted professional, freelance designers provide a final product as the deliverable.

Instead of delivering photographic prints, I deliver a file that may be sent to the printer. The file I've provided is the deliverable or final product you are purchasing.

Some people call this *"first reproduction rights"* or *"one-time reproduction rights"*, meaning you, the client, may take the final artwork to the printer and have it reproduced by professional printers. Does that make sense?

Client: Sort of, but I thought that when I paid you I got everything.

You: Think of it this way: When you work with a professional photographer, perhaps for a family portrait, you pay for a particular package and receive your photographs rather than the negatives. Coincidentally, if the photographer does provide the negatives she/he will always charge for them — right?

When you hire a designer like me, you pay for the final product rather than the rights to the master digital files, which would allow you or anyone else to edit the artwork.
Does that clear things up?

For good or ill, your conversation is your advertisement. Every time you open your mouth you let men look into your mind. Do they see it well clothed, neat, business wise?
— Bruce Burton

Why do *quick copy places* let me have these master files but you won't?

Client is REALLY saying this to you, "I have found other design shops (other freelancers) that give out files; why don't you? I want you to change your policy."

You: If a quick copy place or freelancer does let you have the files, they have probably built the cost of relinquishing all rights to the artwork into the price you paid. I've found that designers (particularly young or inexperienced ones) often don't know how the industry works, so they mistakenly give away files.

Client: Okay, but why would they provide the files when you won't?

You: The American Institute of Graphic Arts, one of the governing boards and a leader in the industry, has this to say on the subject:

"Graphic artists, like photographers, writers and other creators, customarily sell only specific rights to the use of their creative work... Some inexperienced art buyers assume that they are buying a product for a flat fee, with the right to reuse or manipulate the art however they wish." — The Graphic Artists Guild Handbook — Pricing and Ethical Guidelines, 9th ed.

Client: If I want the files how do I get them?

You: You'll find that some freelancing professionals won't even consider providing these files to you. However, this is something that I will provide to clients if specifically requested. It's billed as a separate cost. I will need to prepare the files, burn them onto a disk and transfer them over to you. Is that something you might be interested in having me do?

NOTE: Of course it's up to you whether or not you want to sell the client the master files. While this might seem like quick, easy money, it can be a host of problems that you might not have anticipated. Clients may expect you to provide technical support with the files, they may screw them up and expect you to replace them, or they may hire another freelancer to work on them and expect you to "coach" them through it. If you need assistance in developing a contract that will protect you, check out *"Work Smarter NOT Harder Contracts and More Package"* on the *Being a Starving Artist Sucks* blog at http://beingastarvingartistsucks.typepad.com

Can't you show me how to makes changes and improvements to the artwork and allow me to do it myself?

Client is REALLY saying this to you, "I don't want to have to pay you for doing the changes. I'd like to see if I can save money by doing them myself."

You: It is possible, but it's going to take a considerable amount of time and money.

Client: How much time and money? I thought it would be easy.

You: We first need to get you set up with professional software, which can run you about $500 - $3000, depending on what you need.

Client: Wow, that's a lot. Can't I get it cheaper?

You: You can probably pick it up on eBay, but you never know what you're going to end up with, right? You'll need the master files from me, which I do provide at an additional charge. You'll want to budget about $500 for them.

Next, we'll need to schedule a time for me to come down to your office and work with you on this. You'll want to block out between 3-5 hours. I am estimating the cost of the training to be around $200 - $450, and maybe an additional 2 hours at a later time to recap anything you might have forgotten or need help with.

If you had additional challenges or questions, I would charge you $45 per hour to provide technical or software support when you need it. Do you think this direction might be a good fit for you, or would you rather just have me make the fixes quickly for you and just pay for my time?

OR:

You: It is possible. Are you interested in learning how to become a freelance designer?

Client: Not really. I just wanted see if this option would save me some time or money.

You: In that case, this option might be more costly than you realize. You could go this route, but you'll need to purchase professional software. I would sell you the master digital files for a reasonable amount so you could edit them, and you'd have to pay for the training.

I've had a number of clients inquire about this before, so it's a good question. All of them have decided that it was much more cost-effective and less hassle to have me do what I do best and help them. Knowing this, what do you think is going to be the best option for you?

NOTE: You've probably already guessed it — this move is designed to scare the client a little bit, or at least give them an idea how much time and expense is going to be required. When most clients ask this question they don't realize just how much time and money it takes.

RA

I know I might not be able to make future changes, but what if I got someone else to do it?

Client is REALLY saying this to you, "What if I find someone better or cheaper than you. Do I still have to hire you?"

You: I'd love to continue to work with you, and I think you'll find I am probably the best person to work on the project since I created it. But you're always welcome to work with another designer if you like.

Client: I probably won't. I just wanted to know if I could.

You: I understand. In this case you'll want to purchase the rights to the master digital files. These are billed as a separate cost and I really only provide them when a client has made a special request for them.

Client: Why will I need to purchase the master files?

You: Once you have these master files, you or anyone else will be able to edit the original artwork. The files that I provided to you at the completion of this project were called *"first reproduction rights"*, which is a fancy way of saying you'll have the ability to reprint this artwork as many times as you'd like, but you won't be able to make changes to it.

Client: I didn't know that. I still might want the files though.

You: Clients sometimes have questions in this area, so I make sure I specifically address it in all my proposals. I think you'll be able to find this on page 3 of our agreement.

If you still would like the files, we can talk about how we'll move forward. There are certain things we'll need to agree to before we would go ahead with this (such as authorship, displaying in a portfolio and technical support), but this is an option.

I'd like to retain your business — how can I make it easier to continue to work with me on this project, and or future ones?

OPTIONAL:

You: Is there are reason why you would want someone other than me to work on this project?

NOTE: You'll want to make certain that your contract clearly and specifically addresses this area so the client doesn't have any misunderstandings in regards to your policies.

The time to stop talking is when the other person nods his head affirmatively, but says nothing.

— Henry S. Haskins

Can I reprint my project/artwork if I want?

Client is REALLY saying this to you, "Do I have to contact you or pay you if I just want to reprint these?"

You: You're welcome to reprint these as much as you like. In fact, if you have a relationship with your own printer, you might not even need to contact me to have them redone. These files have been designed according to typical industry standards, so any professional, reputable printer will be able to reproduce these.

Client: Will I get the same quality you got with your printer?

You: If you like the results we got from working with my printer, you may choose to have me handle the job again to make sure you get exactly the results you want. You are welcome to take this artwork to another printer, but understand that your results may vary, not because of the quality of the digital files, but due to the varying expertise of the printer.

Client: Will I be able to change some of the artwork if I like or make some updates to it?

You: In some rare cases, you'll be able to make some minor changes to the artwork, but I wouldn't recommend it unless you have the appropriate software and are extremely comfortable using it.

Client: Okay, but can I have the printer make some changes?

You: Often a printer will have a production artist on staff that can help you in a very limited capacity, but I've seen first hand that this can cause more harm than good. In all honesty, I would recommend that you have me make the changes for you so that you know you don't end up with unwelcome surprises.

Since I created the file, I am familiar with it, and I will be able to make most changes quickly and efficiently. You may find that if your printer's designer makes changes, you'll end up with two different files that have been printed, which can cause confusion.

Unless you want to learn graphic design or there's a specific reason why you wouldn't want me to work on these files, it might be worth your time and effort just to let me handle it for you.
Besides, I enjoy working with you!

SECTION VI:
Do Your Clients Pass the Test?
A Quick and Easy Rating System

"I cannot divine how it happens that the man who knows the least is the most argumentative."

**— Giovani della Casa,
1503-1556, Papal Secretary of State**

Do Your Clients Pass the Test
A Quick & Easy Rating System

Whether it's a client, a sibling or even a romantic interest, people have difficulty seeing how others really treat them.

Have you ever had a friend who is dating someone that's clearly wrong for them, but he or she just can't see it? People often develop blind spots (in critical areas of their personal and professional life) that cloud their vision as well as their judgment. In talking with freelancers, I've observed the same phenomenon when it comes to their clients.

I've learned that some freelancers see all of their clients as good — even some of the rotten ones (which is amazing to me). On the other hand, I've also met designers who felt that all of their clients were bad even though some of them didn't sound like it.

This got me thinking about how to come up with a way, even if it were just for fun, to determine if a client was someone I wanted to keep around or not. While there might not be a "written in stone" formula for determining a good/bad client, I came up with some pretty good criteria based on my own experiences as well as feedback I gathered from other creative freelancers.

If you have doubts about whether or not you want to continue to work with a client, put them through the test on the following pages and see how they do.

I should point out that while this exercise can give you some good insights about your clients, it's also meant to be fun. You should base whether or not to work with a client on: how much work you currently have, how much you need money, if you like the projects the client gives you, if you can tolerate the client, if the client is likely to give you more work or referrals, etc.

Lastly, I encourage you to add to this list with your own criteria — I am sure you'll be able to come up with some of your own ways to measure clients as well; use what I have here as a benchmark.

For each of the statements below, select Strongly Disagree, Disagree, Neutral, Agree or Strongly Agree.

You'll receive 0 points for Strongly Disagree, 1 for Disagree, 2 for Neutral, 3 for Agree and 4 for Strongly Agree.

Scoring is a lot like golf: you want to have a low score rather than high. The higher the score, the worse the client...in theory anyway.

	SD	D	N	A	SA
My client often asks me to work overtime or weekends in order to meet his or her deadlines	○	○	○	○	○
My client often argues, complains, or haggles on price.	○	○	○	○	○
I catch my client saying, "I'm not sure what's wrong with it. It just needs something," but they don't know what that "something" is.	○	○	○	○	○
My client sometimes curses at me, insults me, or belittles me.	○	○	○	○	○
I feel like my client always seems stressed out, which in turn stresses me out.	○	○	○	○	○
My client has disappeared in the middle of a project, leaving me to chase them down.	○	○	○	○	○
I feel like my client always has rush projects, but is unwilling to pay for them.	○	○	○	○	○
I feel that my client sometimes takes advantage of my policy to keep working on a project until I make them happy.	○	○	○	○	○
Rather than providing constructive criticism, my client says things like, "I don't like this", "This is not good", or "This isn't what I want."	○	○	○	○	○
My client forgets to, avoids, or always has an excuse for why he or she can't pay me on time.	○	○	○	○	○

How many points did your client score?

00 - 12: Just better than working for Dracula, consider firing or garlic.

13 - 24: Stay with them short-term, look to replace them long-term.

25 - 40: Not the best in the world, but you can work with them.

41 - 50: You've got a gem, do what you have to keep them.

Okay you've probably had some fun finding out how good...or bad your clients are (based on the scoring system), but you can actually take that exercise and put it to good use in finding better clients.

Step back and analyze the clients you put through the previous exercise and ask these questions:

1. What do my good/bad clients have in common (age, gender, income level, personality, budget, profession, value systems, etc.)?
2. How do my good/bad clients find me (referral, advertisement, internet, etc.)?
3. Why do my good/bad clients decide to hire me (hopefully you've asked them this when they hire you)?
4. What is it about my good/bad clients that makes them good or bad?
5. As I look at all of this information, what commonalities do I see with my good clients versus my bad clients? In knowing what makes a client a good one, how should I adjust my marketing in the future to attract more of them?

Whether you're fishing or trying to attract new clients, the practice is the same: **learn everything you can about what you're trying to catch and devise an approach that will allow you to catch them**. For example, if you like catfish and not scrod, you should invest time in learning what approaches and lures attract catfish but not scrod. If you find that most of your good clients come from referrals and the bad ones come from online advertising, you'll want to invest resources in developing a referral program and reduce your online advertising budget.

By investing a little time in determining what makes a client good or bad, you're be arming yourself with knowledge that will help you catch the good ones and leave the bad ones — a great use of your time!

賢

SECTION VII:
Additional Resources and Information

Conclusion

Recommended Resources for Designers

Acknowledgements

About the Author

Sharing, Copyright and Distribution

Index of Verbal Choke Holds

Conclusion

What You Should Take Away from Verbal Kung Fu for Freelancers

I hope you'll be taking away some value from reading this book, and that you've enjoyed it. I've enjoyed sharing it with you. Here are a few quick points I wanted to leave you with as you take what you've learned and apply it to your freelancing business.

Remember, the focus of *Verbal Kung Fu for Freelancers* is not to manipulate or take advantage of your clients but to find an effective, fair way to communicate and find resolution. By going through this book you've found a new confidence and a power with your words — use them wisely and ethically.

Rather than feeling like you have to memorize all of these "comebacks", focus on learning the technique of *Verbal Kung Fu for Freelancers*. Listen, empathize, offer a solution, and wait for a response. If you practice regularly and make a conscious effort to get more comfortable responding to people, you may also find that *Verbal Kung Fu* can be applied to your personal relationships as well!

Use *Verbal Kung Fu for Freelancers* as a framework for what to say and how to say it, but **use your own words when responding to people**. If one of my responses doesn't feel or sound right to you (or it's just not how you'd say it), feel free to change things around so it does. It's important that your responses are natural and authentic to you — make sure you respond in a way that's comfortable to you.

Lastly, I'd like to congratulate you on taking steps to improve yourself and the success of your freelancing business — nice work!

I thank you for purchasing this book and allowing me to share my experiences with you. I'll be praying that you reach the freelancing goals you've set out to achieve; I hope this book will be instrumental in helping you to get there.

Be sure to find some small way today of rewarding yourself for finishing this book and getting your black belt in *Verbal Kung Fu for Freelancers*. Gōngxi gōngxi (Chinese for "Congratulations").

PS - For those familiar with Asian culture or living in Asia, I realize that I have an unusual mix of Japanese and Chinese themes in this book. For example: Kung Fu's origin in Chinese, yet I've used Japanese kanji and referred to the martial arts master as, "sensei", which is also Japanese. This was done for the sake of simplicity and familiarity, and not meant as an offense to anyone's heritage.

Best Wishes and God Bless.

For my friend and mentor, Bill Gluth, who provided the inspiration for honing my Verbal Kung Fu skills and writing this book.

RA
Illustration of me

When all is said and done, success without happiness is the worst kind of failure.

- Louis Binstock
  American Minister

Like this Book? Check Out These Other Creative Freelancer Resources

http://beingastarvingartistsucks.typepad.com

The Creative Freelance Designer's Audio Success Series: (MP3s)

Created to help address the tricky situations that cause designers the most stress and difficulties. Asking for referrals, telling a client they're asking for too many revisions and negotiating the best price for yourself - there are 8 tracks in all...over 2 hours of invaluable, no-fluff insights and strategies that will give you a competitive edge.

'Work Smarter NOT Harder' Contracts and More Package

A comprehensive package of over 20+ email templates, questionnaires and contracts that all freelancers should have in their arsenal. These are documents Jeremy's developed and used for years. A must for any talented designer who wants to invest more time creating and less time doing administrative work, or worrying if their contract and client communications sound professional.

Being a Starving Artist Sucks

Creative freelance designers have called this book "The Bible" of graphic design business success. Geared towards helping aspiring as well as experienced creative designers realize their dream of running a profitable, professional freelancing business, this resource is filled with expert advice and insider strategies in the areas that all designers struggle with. 500 pages, fully illustrated, easy to read - it's like Jeremy is right there guiding you. Available on Amazon.com or the iTunes App Store.

* These are digital files rather than disks but who uses disks anymore?

Acknowledgements

Illustrations

The illustrations in Verbal Kung Fu for Freelancers were drawn by three outstanding freelancers: Carlos Ponce, Matthew Hein and Rich Arnold.

Carlos Ponce is a talented illustrator and polished graphic communicator with more than 20 years of experience in graphic design and Illustration.

He has received numerous awards and acknowledgements from the International Salon of Cartoons, Montreal, Canada, and Cartoon Competition Against the Use of Drugs, sponsored by the Mexican Government's Attorney General, to mention just a few.

Email: carlos@freelat.com
Skype ID: poncecarlos248
Web site: http://poncecarlos.elance.com

Matthew Hein is an aspiring digital artist who specializes in digital illustration and computer graphics. As a graduate from the Art Institute of Phoenix, Matt hopes to launch his career as a professional digital artist and work on a wide variety of exciting projects.

Matt utilizes a variety of software programs in his work, including 3DS Max, Flash and Photoshop.

He is also an avid photographer and spends much of his free time hiking and shooting photos of the Arizona landscape.

http://www.matthewhein.com

Rich Arnold of RWA Graphics is an accomplished illustrator, cartoonist, animator and graphic designer. His career focus is on creating digital graphics and animation for marketing, educational, and entertainment content delivered via Internet or local networks.

Rich has the unique ability to provide clients with an incredible range of styles, from corporate to hysterically funny. As the sole illustrator for the first ground-breaking book in this series, *Being a Starving Artist Sucks*, Rich created over 50 cartoons that have received both acclaim and big laughs.

His illustrations are featured in both the *Being a Starving Artist Sucks* and *Verbal Kung Fu for Freelancers* logos.

Email: arnold@rwagraphics.com
Web site: www.rwagraphics.com

Editing

- Scott R. Quakkelaar
- Lindsay Tuber
- Craig Condit (iPhone platform developer as well)
- Eric & Amber Hartmann, Two Turtles Multimedia, Inc

Strategy / Marketing

Bill Gluth, Next Level Strategic Marketing Specialists and Creating Words that Sell.
www.nextlevelsalesandmarketing.com

Wondering why there are three illustrators instead of one? This book was created to help as many creative freelancers worldwide as possible. With that spirit in mind, I felt giving three deserving illustrators the chance to showcase their skills was better than one.

About the Author

Being a business savvy designer is often a contradiction in terms; however, Jeremy Tuber is a unique combination of savvy business marketer and creative designer. This one-two punch provides his clients with targeted marketing and design projects that yield outstanding results and a terrific return on their investment. A self taught, self-motivated designer, Jeremy worked his way out of the corporate world close to ten years ago to pursue his true passion in design, studying and learning the profession from the bottom up. Starting at a local Kinkos store and moving from design position to design position over the course of a few years – each one a bit more rewarding than the last, he's had the good fortune of working in many design environments with well over a hundred different artists.

This unique perspective of being creative and business savvy, along with extensive practical experience in the corporate world has given him an exceptional advantage in understanding the marketing/design challenges and needs of business owners. Jeremy's been called a walking, talking ad agency - he's a marketing manager and a creative director in one package.

Jeremy has a decade of experience with brand identity, web design, marketing strategy, advertising creations, direct mail, content editing, custom photography, photo editing/manipulation, and multimedia presentations.

As a published author with 60 + articles to his credit, Jeremy enjoys providing value and education to creative freelancers and small business owners looking to bring in more sales and "*take their business to the next level*." He has been invited to speak to art students/alumni at local colleges, including the Art Institute of Phoenix. He continues to develop insightful resources to give designers an opportunity to make their dream of running a creative freelancing business a reality: the '*Work Smarter NOT Harder*' *Contracts Package*, *The Creative Freelance Designer's Audio Success Series (MP3s)* and his first break-through book, *Being a Starving Artist Sucks*.

Sharing, Copyright and Distribution

If I've provided some good information to you with this book, I would ask that you **please** do not file share it with others who have not paid for it. For the amount of value in the book, I am not asking a lot in return.

Creative freelancers that are truly serious about becoming successful will have no trouble affording this book. By skipping that morning latte for a few of weeks, they'd have enough money to afford this resource, and it'll pay for itself by bringing on just one client.

I've made resources on the web site available for free distribution; you'll also find additional free tips on the Being a Starving Artist Sucks/Verbal Kung Fu for Freelancers Blog. This copy is meant for you only.

I appreciate your honoring this copyright — as freelancers we just want to be paid fairly for our creativity.

Best wishes!

Jeremy Tuber
Mentor, Resource and Educator to Creative Freelance Designers Everywhere

Index
Quick Reference to Find a Specific Verbal Choke Hold

- If you help us with this project we'll be able to bring in some revenue and pay you some money...**40**

- If you can give us a price break on this project, we'll pay you extra on the next...**42**

- My budget is $500, firm...**43**

- I am not sure what my budget is...**44**

- Is there another way we can work this out?...**45**

- Is there something we can do about the price?...**46**

- I am looking for someone to partner with on this project. You'll get a portion of the profits...**47**

- I'd like to work with you, but I've received bids from other designers and they are less expensive...**48**

- Why should I pay you to design my web site when I can just get a template or go through an automated online system?...**50**

- I am having several freelancers come in to interview. I'd like you to come in too. Are you available?...**52**

- Can you send me a proposal and let me think it over?...**54**

- I'd like to set up another meeting with you to talk about how you can help me...**55**

- I'd just like to set up a meeting where I can learn about you and get some ideas on where to go with my business...**56**

- Mock up something, and if I like it I'll pay you...**58**

- Why don't you design something, and if we like it we'll hire you...**59**

- I am not sure now if we even need this project. Maybe we shouldn't move forward...**60**

- You'll meet with my assistant and he or she will give me the details about you and the project later...**61**

- Drop off your mock-ups or sketches and we'll decide later if we want to hire you...**62**

- Why don't you look at what I have and what my competitors offer, and then give me some ideas?...**63**

- Let me talk to my business partner before we move forward with a commitment to hire you...**64**

- Before I hire you for this project, I'd like to call some of your past clients and talk to them about you...**64**

- I noticed you haven't been in business that long...**65**

- I just need you to work up some prices for me and I'll decide later...**66**

- I always get 3-5 price quotes before making a decision (or I am still looking around at other options). When I've made up my mind I'll let you know...**68**

- I'd like to see more examples than what you have on your web site. Can I see more?...**68**

- I am interested in using your services, but I am going to have to put it on hold for the time being. I have some money coming in and as that happens; I will probably use your services down the road...**70**

- Client does not respond at all after you've sent over a proposal. Even after following up, the client doesn't return phone calls or emails...**71**

- I'd like to get together and just talk about this project a little bit. When would be a good time?...**72**

- I just found out that my grandfather is very ill and I need to pay for plane tickets back home. We need to put the project on hold until I've had a chance to sort things out here and find enough money to pay you...**74**

- I am not Jewish, I am just spiritual. Is that going to be a problem?...**75**

- I don't have time to proof the advertisement. I am sure it's fine; go ahead and send it to the printer...*110*

- I know we approved the current design, but we asked a few of our friends and they have suggested some changes...*112*

- Can you contact my web host and help me sort this out?...*114*

- Will I be able to contact you after hours or on weekends if I need to?...*116*

- I don't have the materials you need, so you will have to get the files from my previous freelancer...*116*

- Can you come in for a meeting at my office?...*118*

- Can you take a look at the text on my web site and make any corrections that you see?...*118*

- I have some pictures to use in the project. Can you scan them in or do some retouching?...*119*

- It's pretty easy to upload video to the internet, right? Can you do that for me?...*120*

- Can you help me figure out why my computer is crashing?...*121*

- Can we swap out some of the stock photos you used in my project?...*122*

- Hey, you deal with computers, can you tell me why my laptop can't connect to the internet?...*123*

- In your "*infinite wisdom*" as a talented freelancer, I'm guessing this will probably only take you about 5 minutes, right?...*124*

- We pay people on the first of each month. You need to talk to the accounts payable department to get paid...*125*

- I need these business cards to go to the printer today, and I'll pay you in next month's billing cycle...*126*

- I never pay a cent until we see the final product...or, Send over the final files and we'll issue a check...**127**

- The check is in the mail; I don't know why you haven't received it...**128**

- When my venture capital comes in, I'll be able to get some money to you...**129**

- I need to handle these bills first and then I can pay you...**131**

- If I put the check in the mail today, will you be able to send out the artwork?...**132**

- I can't pay you up front. I need to be able to make payments on the balance or I have to go elsewhere...**133**

- The colors on my brochure came out dull or different compared to my computer screen. What can be done about this?...**134**

- My project didn't get done when I needed it, so I don't think I should pay for it...**136**

- I need to make a change to the artwork. I know it's been sent to the printer, but is there anything we can do?...**137**

- I have a deadline, so I need you to call the printer and get them to run my job right now...**138**

- What if I want to make changes to my project in the future?...**140**

- I've already paid you for the work, so why don't I get it?...**141**

- Why do quick copy places let me have these master files but you won't? ...**142**

- Can't you show me how to makes changes and improvements to the artwork and allow me to do it myself?...**143**

- I know I might not be able to make future changes, but what if I got someone else to do it?...**144**

- Can I reprint my project/artwork if I want?...**146**

耶穌基督

Rev 3:20